# Revise for Religious Studies GCSE for AQA Specification A

## Gordon Geddes and Jane Griffiths

Heinemann Educational Publishers
Halley Court, Jordan Hill, Oxford OX2 8EJ
Part of Harcourt Education Limited

Heinemann is a registered trademark of Harcourt Education Limited

© Gordon Geddes and Jane Griffiths, 2003

First published 2003

07 06 05 04 03
10 9 8 7 6 5 4 3 2

British Library Cataloguing in Publication Data is available from the British Library on request.

ISBN 0 435 30698 7

Designed by Artistix, Thame

Typeset by Saxon Graphics Ltd, Derby

Original illustrations © Harcourt Education Limited, 2003

Printed and bound in the UK by Bath Press Ltd

Cover photo: © Sonia Halliday

Picture research by Jennifer Johnson

**Acknowledgements**

The publishers would like to thank the following for permission to reproduce copyright material: AQA examination questions reproduced by permission of the Assessment and Qualifications Alliance. Tearfund, p. 111, www.tearfund.org, 0845 -355-8355.

The publishers would like to thank the following for permission to use photographs: Andes PA/Carlos Reyes-Manzo, pp. 53 (both), 60, 69, 76, 129, 136, 145 and 150; Rex Features/Scott Laperruque, p. 116; Rex Features/Brian Strickland, p. 122; TRIP, p. 115; TRIP/A Tovy, p. 86; TRIP/J Ringland, p. 70; Walking Camera, p. 81; www.springharvest.org, p. 91.

Every effort has been made to contact copyright holders of material reproduced in this book. Any omissions will be rectified in subsequent printings if notice is given to the publishers.

Tel: 01865 888058 www.heinemann.co.uk

# Contents

# How to use this book

## Welcome!

*Revise for Religious Studies GCSE for AQA A* has been written to help you revise successfully for your Religious Studies GCSE.

## Which options are you studying?

You will be studying two options. Your first option will be one of these:

| 1A | Christianity |
| 1B | Christian Belief and Practice with reference to the Roman Catholic Tradition |
| 1C | The Christian Life and St. Mark's Gospel |
| 1D | Christianity and the Synoptic Gospels. |

Your second option will be one of these:

| 2A | Effects of Christianity on Behaviour, Attitudes and Lifestyles |
| 2B | Effects of the Roman Catholic Tradition on Aspects of Christian Lifestyle and Behaviour |

**Specification areas are clearly indicated at the top of each section.**

You may find it useful to mark in some way the sections which are relevant to the options you are studying. Many sections are relevant to more than one option. Again, mark the parts of the section which you need to study for your option.

Many passages are relevant to more than one part of a specification. These passages are only covered once in this book. Elsewhere you will find the direction 'See page 00' or 'Read more'. If you cannot remember the passage, turn to that page and read about it.

In some cases, Bible passages come in more than one option, under more than one topic. The passage may be explained in a section which is not in your option and so there is a cross-reference to that page.

Many of the Bible passages have been summarized for you. However, you must read the set Bible passages for yourself.

## Your course

Each section begins with a 'Topic summary' and 'What do I need to know?' These give an outline of the information you will need to answer examination questions on the topic, including relevant Bible references.

## Key words

Important words and terms are in bold print. The definitions can be found in the glossary on pages 158–9.

## Did you know?

These short pieces of information are useful additions to your knowledge and can be used as examples in examination answers.

## Hints and tips

These are brief guidelines which are designed to assist revision and examination technique.

## Beware!

These are tips to help you avoid commonly made mistakes in the examination.

## Read more

These highlight extra Bible passages you may wish to read and learn to add more detail to your answers. They may also direct you to another section of the book where passages are explained in more detail or, where there is a choice of examples to study (such as one of a number of aid agencies), they may suggest you look again at those you studied during your course.

# Questions

There are questions at the end of each section. Most have been taken from past AQA examination papers.

- **Try these short questions.** These will give you examination practice and a good indication as to whether you have revised in sufficient detail. Answers can be found on pages 155–7.
- **Exam-type questions.** Student answers to these questions are given, followed by an examiner's comment and mark. They include points about examination technique and the correct strategy for answering the questions.
- **Examination practice.** These questions are for you to think about and try on your own.

# How to tackle questions which test your knowledge and understanding

- Often you will be asked to describe something. Assume that the examiner will take nothing for granted. For instance, if you are describing the iconostasis in an Orthodox church (page 81) and you simply put: 'It separates the congregation from the sanctuary', the examiner may realize that you know it is a screen, but may not credit you for knowing it. You must say it is a screen.
- Look out for words like 'explain'. They are a sign to you that you are being asked, for example, not only to describe what happens but also to explain why it happens.
- You may sometimes be given a choice within a question. For example: 'Describe the work of an agency which offers long term aid to developing countries.' You must name the agency.
- When a question is based on a picture, study it carefully. It is there as an aid, even if the question does not refer directly to it.

# How to tackle evaluation questions

- Some questions are structured in a way to show that your evaluation skills – your own judgment – are being tested.
- Very often the question begins with a statement in quotation marks. The statement is followed by something like: 'Do you agree? Give reasons for your answer showing that you have thought about more than one point of view.'
- You will not be given marks just for saying 'Yes' or 'No' – even if the examiner agrees with you!
- You are being assessed for the sort of reasons you give. You must look at two or more approaches to the question, perhaps from different points of view.
- You may not be able to decide whether you fully agree with the statement. This may be a good sign. You may see what is good and bad about both sides of the argument. Make sure that you say what the strong and the weak points are on either side of the argument.

# Finally, some hints on revision

- Start your final revision at least two months before your examination.
- Pick out the sections from this book that are part of your course.
- Do not just read through all the sections in one go. Decide that you will read a certain number each week. Work through them carefully, one at a time.
- Make sure you know the Bible passages well. Even when they are summarized in this book, read the passages themselves.
- You may have studied examples for some topics – for example, worship, aid agencies, notable Christians – which are not the ones chosen in this book. Revise the examples you have learned during your course.
- Remember the **Checklist for revision** at the end of each section.

# 1 Background to the Gospels

## Topic summary

- The Jews longed for God to fulfil his promise of a **Messiah** who would set them free from their enemies and lead them to a closer relationship with God.

- The **Gospel** writers believed that God had fulfilled his promise in the person of Jesus. They wrote their Gospels to convince people that Jesus is the Son of God.

- Each Gospel writer had his own reasons for writing and his own sources of information. However, the Gospels of Matthew, Mark and Luke are similar enough in detail to be called **synoptic**.

## What do I need to know?

- The political and religious situation at the time of Jesus.
- What is a Gospel? Why were the Gospels written?
- Ways in which Christians look upon the Bible as the Word of God – literalism, fundamentalism, conservative view, liberal view.
- **1C** Who was Mark? Why did he write his Gospel? What sources did he use?
- **1D** In what ways are the Gospels of Matthew, Mark and Luke different from each other? Why are they different?

## The Jews – God's chosen people

The Jews believed

- in the existence of one God, who alone should be worshipped
- they were the chosen people of God
- God had given them the land of Canaan, later known as Palestine
- they had a special **covenant** relationship with God in which they promised to **worship** him alone and follow his **commandments**. In return, God would protect and love them
- one day God would send them the Messiah.

## Roman occupation

In 63BC the Romans invaded Palestine and it became part of the Roman Empire. The emperor allowed Herod the Great, who was partly Jewish, to rule as a 'puppet king'. He was unpopular because the Jews felt that he obeyed the Romans too readily.

After the death of Herod the Great, Palestine was divided among his three sons. Later the emperor replaced one of Herod's sons, Archelaus, with procurators (governors) to rule Judaea. In AD26, Pontius Pilate became procurator.

**did you know?**

Herod was king when Jesus was born; he is the Herod visited by the Magi (Matthew 2: 1–11).

Being conquered by the Romans was a tremendous blow to the Jewish people. God's chosen people were now ruled by people who did not believe in God. Their whole way of life was in danger. When would God send his promised Messiah?

On the title 'Messiah', page 18

## Religious life

At the time of Jesus, the temple in Jerusalem was the centre of worship for Jews all over the world. Started by Herod the Great in 20BC, it was not completed until AD64, over 30 years after Jesus' death. It was destroyed by the Romans six years later and was never rebuilt. The temple was the house of God. The Holy of Holies in the centre of the temple was the place where God was thought to be particularly present. Only the High Priest could enter the Holy of Holies and even he could only go there on the Day of Atonement each year.

The temple was the only place where **sacrifices** could be offered to God. Jews, wherever they lived in the world, tried to visit the temple at least once a year, especially for the festival of Passover.

In the synagogue Jews met to worship God and to study the **scriptures**. After the destruction of the temple, synagogues became the main places of worship.

## Religious groups

Jesus often came into contact with the main religious groups of his day. Most of them saw Jesus as a threat to their teachings and way of life.

- *The Sadducees* were a party of priests who controlled worship at the temple. They were wealthy and held high status in Jewish society. They believed that the Law of Moses (the Torah) contained all the laws necessary for leading a good life. They did not believe in a life after death, in angels, or that God would send a Messiah.

  The Sadducees had a good relationship with the Romans. They agreed to keep the peace among the Jewish people and, in return, the Romans gave them freedom to lead the worshipping lives of the Jews.

- *The Pharisees* had a great deal of influence in the synagogues and in every Jewish community. They devoted their lives to studying the Torah. To make sure that God's commandments were followed in daily life they created many extra rules on matters such as washing, eating, the **Sabbath** and festivals. Jesus said that the Pharisees had created too many laws, making the religious life a burden rather than a joy.

  The title 'Pharisee' means 'separated one'. The Pharisees believed that, to remain religiously clean, Jews should separate themselves from foreigners and social outcasts so they had few dealings with their Roman conquerors. They believed in a life after death and the coming of God's promised Messiah.

- *The Scribes* were trained over many years to copy God's Word clearly and without error. Through their work, they became experts on the Jewish Law and made their own interpretations.

**did you know?**

All that remains today of the temple in Jerusalem is the Western Wall. It is often called 'The Wailing Wall', as Jewish pilgrims mourn there for the loss of the temple, the house of God.

- *The Sanhedrin*, meaning 'council', was the supreme court of the Jews and was led by the High Priest. Members included priests (Sadducees), Pharisees, Scribes and Elders (leading citizens of Jerusalem). The Sanhedrin had the power to pass religious laws and punish those who broke the Jewish Law. They also helped the Romans to keep order. After the Romans conquered Palestine, the Sanhedrin lost the right to execute those who broke the Law. For this reason Jesus was brought before Pontius Pilate, who alone had the right to sentence someone to death.

**hints and tips**
You will not be asked directly to answer questions on the religious and political situation at the time of Jesus. However, the information above will help you understand what life was like at the time of Jesus.

## The Gospels

In the New Testament, there are four Gospels – Matthew, Mark, Luke and John. The word 'Gospel' means 'good news'. The Gospels proclaimed the good news about Jesus. In the opening verse of his Gospel, Mark explains the good news well – Jesus is the Christ, the promised Messiah. He is also the Son of God (Mark 1: 1). The Gospels were written to describe the ministry, death and **resurrection** of Jesus and to help others realize how these events affected their lives. They are very important to Christians because they contain almost all that is known about Jesus.

### Why was the life of Jesus written down?

In the first years after the resurrection, the news about Jesus was passed on by word of mouth. Many had seen and heard Jesus personally. They believed that Jesus would return in their own lifetimes to establish the **kingdom of God** – their priority was to pass on the good news about Jesus as quickly as possible. As time passed, the need for a written record of Jesus' life became clear.

- People who had known Jesus well were dying. It was important to write down their memories before they were forgotten.
- Converts to Christianity needed a written record of Jesus' life and teachings to strengthen their **faith**.
- The story of Jesus had to be accurate, free from exaggeration and distortion.
- Christians were being persecuted for their belief in Jesus. They needed encouragement to face their suffering.

**did you know?**

'Synoptic' means view together.

The first three Gospels are called synoptic because they give a similar picture of Jesus.

## Mark's Gospel

This was probably the first Gospel to be written around AD65, 30 years after the death of Jesus. No one is sure who Mark was, but several clues are given in the New Testament and other early writings.

- He could have been a companion of Paul (Acts 13:1–13).
- He could have been the Mark mentioned by Peter in his first letter (1 Peter 5: 13).
- Some think that he was the naked young man in the Garden of Gethsemane on the night of Jesus' arrest (Mark 14: 51–2).
- Papias (an early Christian writer) says that Mark was a close friend of the apostle Peter and a recorder of Peter's memories.

When writing his Gospel, Mark would have had a number of sources of information:

- oral **tradition** – information about Jesus passed on by word of mouth in the memories, conversations and teaching of the early Christians
- the memories of Peter
- eye-witness accounts of those who had seen and heard Jesus
- early collections of teachings about Jesus written by the first Christian preachers
- Old Testament prophecies about the Messiah.

## Characteristics of Mark's Gospel  1C

*The healing of blind Bartimaeus (Mark 10: 46–52) may well be based on an eye witness account.*

- The Gospel contains Jesus' Galilean ministry, his journey to Jerusalem, his final week, his crucifixion and resurrection. A large proportion of the Gospel is dedicated to the final week of Jesus' life and his death.
- It was written for **Gentiles**, perhaps for Christians living in Rome. He explains Jewish customs and translates Jesus' **Aramaic** words into Greek (for example, 'Talitha koum!' Mark 5: 41).
- Mark portrays Jesus as a man of action. He performs **miracles**, forgives sins and exorcises evil spirits. There is less emphasis on Jesus' teaching.
- The miracles are signs of God's power working through Jesus and of the coming of the kingdom of God.
- Mark uses these titles to describe Jesus – 'Son of Man', 'Messiah' and 'Son of God'.
- The **disciples** are often shown in a bad light. They fail to understand Jesus' teachings, they make mistakes and they abandon Jesus in his time of need.
- **Key verse:** 'For even the Son of Man did not come to be served, but to serve, and to give his life as a ransom for many.' (Mark 10: 45)

## Characteristics of Matthew's Gospel  1D

- The Gospel was written around AD70–80. It was written for Jewish Christians and is the most Jewish in nature of all the Gospels.
- The author wished to show his readers that Jesus was the Messiah. He uses passages from the scriptures, particularly in the birth story, to prove that Jesus fulfilled the promises made by the Old Testament prophets.
- Matthew uses Jewish titles – 'Messiah', 'Son of David', 'King of the Jews'.
- Matthew gives little detail of the birth of Jesus. The story is told from Joseph's point of view and includes the visit of the Magi.
- Scholars believe that Matthew copied much of Mark's Gospel and altered it in parts to suit his purposes. He (and Luke) may also have used a source called Q, as well as his own personal material.
- **Key verse:** 'Do not think that I have come to abolish the Law or the Prophets; I have not come to abolish them but to fulfil them.' (Matthew 5: 17)

**did you know?**
Matthew's presentation of Jesus as King has led to some people calling his Gospel, 'The Royal Gospel'.

## Characteristics of Luke's Gospel 1D

- The Gospel was written around AD70–80 by a Gentile. Although he had not met Jesus, Luke would have learnt a great deal about him from Paul. Luke also wrote the Acts of the Apostles.

- In the opening verses of his Gospel, Luke says that he wrote his book to provide his readers with a reliable account of the life of Jesus. He dedicates the Gospel to Theophilus, a name which means 'lover of God'. This could be an individual or any follower of Christ.

- This is a joyful Gospel and begins and ends with **hymns** of praise. Luke is keen to show Jesus' interest and compassion for the outcasts of society, the poor, the sick, women and foreigners. Jesus has come for all people, regardless of race or religion.

- This, more than the other synoptic Gospels, emphasizes the importance and work of the Holy Spirit.

- Jesus is shown at **prayer** more often in Luke's Gospel and teaches in more detail about prayer (for example, The Pharisee and the Tax Collector, Luke 18: 9–14).

- Like Matthew, Luke 'borrowed' large sections from Mark's Gospel. He also used source Q. A number of stories are unique to Luke – **parables** such as the Good Samaritan and the Forgiving Father, and accounts of Jesus' conversations with Zacchaeus and the penitent thief on the cross.

- Luke gives a detailed account of the birth of Jesus from Mary's point of view.

- **Key verse:** 'The Son of Man came to seek and to save what was lost.' (Luke 19: 10)

> **did you know?**
> Luke was a doctor who travelled with Paul on his missionary journeys.

> **did you know?**
> Some scholars think that Matthew and Luke must have got some material from the same source. They call the source Q. No copy of Q exists.

## The Bible as the Word of God

Christians believe that the Bible is the Word of God and that it is relevant for all generations. But what they mean by the term 'Word of God' varies.

- *Fundamentalist Christians* believe that the Bible is **inspired** by God and that those who wrote the books of the Bible were completely directed by God. The Bible contains no errors. Fundamentalists believe, for example, that the miracles happened just as they are written in the Gospels.

- *Literalist Christians* are fundamentalists who take every event and story in the Bible literally. For example, they believe that God created the world in six twenty-four hour periods.

- *Conservative Christians* believe that the Bible is inspired by God. However, they say that the Bible is a spiritual, not a scientific text. At times, it may be difficult to understand a particular passage. They believe that people should look for the meaning behind the words and actions of Jesus.

- *Liberal Christians* believe that the writers of the Bible were guided by God but, as humans, they may have made mistakes. They believe that what is written should not always be taken literally; the events contain spiritual truth in the form of parables, poems and imaginative writings. Liberal Christians do not necessarily believe in the physical resurrection of the body of Christ. What matters to them is the truth that Jesus lives among his followers.

## Try these short questions

**a** What is a covenant? (2 marks)

**b** What was the importance of the temple to the Jews? (3 marks)

**c** Who were the Pharisees? (3 marks)

**d** Give one example of an Aramaic word or phrase used in Mark's Gospel and explain what it means. (3 marks)

## Exam-type questions

**a** What does the word 'Gospel' mean? (1 mark)

**b** Suggest two different ways in which Christians may believe that the Gospels are the 'Word of God'. (4 marks) (SEG, 1996)

### Student's answer

*a   The word 'Gospel' means good news.*

*b   Fundamentalist Christians believe that the Gospel writers were completely inspired by God. Liberal Christians believe that the writers were guided by God when they wrote their Gospels, but that they made mistakes because they were human.*

## Examiner's comments

**a** Correct meaning.

Mark: 1/1

**b** The student has correctly identified two different ways in which Christians believe that the Gospels are the 'Word of God'. However, the answer given is only worth 1 mark in both cases. For a further 2 marks, the student would have to add more detail and perhaps give an illustration from the Gospels. For example, Fundamentalists believe that the Gospels contain no errors; everything is true. Jesus' miracles are completely true in every detail.

Mark: 2/4

## Examination practice

Explain why, for many Christians, it is important that Mark's Gospel is based on eye-witness accounts. (4 marks) (AQA, 2002)

# Checklist for revision

| | Understand and know | Need more revision | Do not understand |
|---|---|---|---|
| I know the importance of the temple and synagogue in the worshipping lives of Jews at the time of Jesus. | ☐ | ☐ | ☐ |
| I understand the work and beliefs of the religious groups at the time of Jesus. | ☐ | ☐ | ☐ |
| I understand how the Gospels came to be written. | ☐ | ☐ | ☐ |
| I know the different characteristics of the synoptic Gospels. | ☐ | ☐ | ☐ |
| I understand how different Christians look upon the Bible as the Word of God. | ☐ | ☐ | ☐ |

# 2 The person of Jesus

## Topic summary

- People asked 'Who is Jesus? What is special about him?'
- The titles used by Jesus himself and by others give insights into the thoughts of Jesus, his followers, his enemies and other people who met him.
- Belief in Jesus is central to Christianity. Christians use what the Gospels say about Jesus as the basis of their belief.

## What do I need to know?

- **1C** The importance of Jesus and the meaning and significance of different titles for Jesus (Son of God, Son of Man, Jesus/Saviour, Christ, **Messiah**, Son of David), both for the **disciples** and for modern Christians.

- **1D** The life of Jesus. The importance of Jesus for Christians today. Some passages given under this heading are covered elsewhere.
  Matthew 14: 22–33 (Walking on the water)
  Mark 4: 35–41 (Calming the storm)
  Mark 5: 21–43 (Jairus' daughter/Woman with internal bleeding)
  Luke 7: 1–10 (Centurion's servant)
  Luke 17: 11–19 (Men with leprosy) – see page 44
  Matthew 12: 9–14 (Healing on the Sabbath) – see page 56

## The birth of Jesus  **1D**

Both Matthew and Luke tell how angels announced that Jesus would be born.

### Luke 1: 26–38. The Annunciation

The angel Gabriel came to Mary at her home in Nazareth. He told her that she was greatly honoured because God had chosen her to have a son, whom she was to name Jesus. He would be the Son of God; his kingdom would never end. Mary was puzzled; how could this happen while she was a virgin? Gabriel replied that the Holy Spirit would cause her to become pregnant and so her child would be the Son of God. Mary accepted God's will in joyful obedience. 'I am the Lord's servant; may it be to me as you have said.'

### Matthew 1: 18–25. Events from Joseph's angle

When he realized that Mary was pregnant he was naturally upset. Rather than humiliate her publicly he decided to end their engagement quietly. The angel told him that Mary's child was from the Holy Spirit. He was to be called Jesus, which means Saviour, because he would save people from their sins. This would fulfil the Old Testament prophecy that a virgin would give birth to a child who would be Emmanuel, a name meaning 'God with us'. Joseph took Mary as his wife but they did not have intercourse before Jesus was born.

### Luke 2: 1–20. Caesar Augustus orders a census

Mary and Joseph had to travel to Bethlehem, since Joseph was descended from David, a great king who had lived 1000 years earlier. Jesus was born and placed in a manger because there was no room in the inn. An angel appeared to shepherds who were with their sheep near Bethlehem. They were frightened, but he told them not to fear. A saviour, the Messiah, had been born in Bethlehem; they would find him in a manger wrapped in swaddling clothes. Many other angels joined him, praising God – 'Glory to God in the highest, and on earth peace to men on whom his favour rests.' The shepherds went to Bethlehem and found everything as the angel had said.

### Matthew 2: 1–12. The visit of the Magi

Magi (wise men or astrologers) came from the east to King Herod in Jerusalem to ask where the new King of the Jews was. They had seen a star from which they had deduced that he had been born. Herod and his court were troubled – a new king of whom they knew nothing was a threat. Herod's advisers told him that according to prophecy the king would be born in Bethlehem. Herod asked the Magi when the star had appeared. He said they were to tell him where the child was so that he could go to worship him. The Magi set off again, overjoyed that the star was still guiding them. They found Jesus and worshipped him. They gave him precious gifts of gold, frankincense and myrrh. They were warned by God in a dream not to return to Herod.

> **did you know?**
>
> The gifts of the Magi are often regarded as signs of who Jesus is: gold for a king, frankincense as an offering to God and myrrh because his death would save those who followed him.

The Magi are important to Christians for two reasons.

1   They were **Gentiles**; their coming was a sign that Jesus was born to save not only Jews but people of all nations.
2   They were great men, yet they came to worship Jesus and to bring him precious gifts – a sign that they realized how great a person this baby was.

## Titles of Jesus  1C  1D

A number of names used for Jesus in the Gospels help Christians understand what Jesus said about himself and what his followers believed about him.

## Son of God

Christians believe that Jesus is the Son of God. Mark makes it clear in the first verse of his **Gospel**: 'The beginning of the Gospel about Jesus Christ, the Son of God.' The title is used by:

● God himself, speaking from heaven. To Christians, this is evidence that Jesus really is the Son of God.
● evil spirits or devils. They would know who Jesus was and fear him.
● the High Priest. He would not believe that Jesus was the Son of God. When Jesus said that he was, the High Priest condemned him to death for **blasphemy**.
● the centurion at the crucifixion, as a sign of respect.

On two occasions a voice was heard from heaven.

## Mark 1: 9–11. The baptism of Jesus

When Jesus was baptized by John the Baptist in the river Jordan a voice came from heaven: 'You are my Son, whom I love; with you I am well pleased.'

## Mark 9: 2–8. The Transfiguration

Jesus took Peter, James and John with him to a high mountain. There, Jesus was transfigured – his appearance changed in a way which made him look awe-inspiring. In the words of Mark's Gospel, 'His clothes became dazzling white, whiter than anyone in the world could bleach them.' Moses and Elijah were there, talking with Jesus. Their appearance would have amazed the three disciples, since they had both been dead for hundreds of years. Moses was the lawgiver, Elijah the greatest of the prophets. They represented two important parts of the religion of the Jews, the Law and the Prophets. Peter asked Jesus if they should build three shelters, for himself, Moses and Elijah – they were so over-awed that they did not really know what to say. Then a voice came from a cloud, 'This is my Son, whom I love. Listen to him!' When they looked, only Jesus was there.

**1D**   Note the next five verses, 9–13. Jesus ordered the three disciples not to tell anyone what had happened until after he had risen from the dead. At that stage they would not have understood what he meant. They talked about the prophecy that Elijah would return before the Messiah came. Jesus replied that Elijah had come already – by which he meant that John the Baptist was the new Elijah.

In a passage from each of **1C** and **1D**, devils or evil spirits call Jesus Son of God. They know who he is and they are afraid of him.

**1C**   ## Mark 1: 21–8. Jesus drives out an evil spirit

The man shouted, 'I know who you are – the Holy One of God.' See page 56.

**1D**   ## Mark 5: 1–20. The man possessed by demons

When Jesus told the evil spirit to leave the man he shouted, 'What do you want with me, Jesus, Son of the Most High God? Swear to God that you won't torture me!' (Different versions of the Bible use different names for the demon – Legion, Mob, Gerasene Demoniac.)

**1C**   **1D**   ## Mark 14: 53–65. Jesus' trial and death

Jesus was condemned to death for saying he was the Son of God. At his trial the High Priest challenged him directly: 'Are you the Christ, the Son of the Blessed One?' Jesus answered, 'I am, and you will see the Son of Man sitting at the right hand of the Mighty One and coming on the clouds of heaven.'

When Jesus died the centurion said, 'Surely this man was the Son of God!' (Mark 15: 39). The centurion was a Roman, not a Jew. Romans believed in many gods; the centurion would not have meant what the High Priest or Jesus meant. Even so, he

To read more about the centurion see page 26.

would have heard people by the cross saying that Jesus said he was the Son of God. His words show that he respected and admired the way Jesus died.

## Son of Man

The title comes from the Old Testament, where Son of Man is sometimes used to describe a heavenly being who has immense power. He is close to the Father and is adored and praised by the angels. In the Gospels the title is used by Jesus himself. Jesus says that the Son of Man

- can forgive sins
- will suffer and die. His death will be a ransom
- will rise again
- will come in glory as judge.

### 1C *Mark 2: 1–12* 1D *Luke 5: 17–26. The healing of the paralysed man*

Jesus was teaching in a house. A paralysed man was brought on his bed, carried by four friends. Since they could not get to the door, they climbed on to the roof, made a hole and lowered the paralysed man to Jesus. Jesus, seeing the faith of the man's friends, said to him, 'Son, your sins are forgiven.'

The teachers of the Law who were present said nothing, but thought, 'He's blaspheming! Who can forgive sins but God alone?' Jesus, knowing what they were thinking, asked, 'Why are you thinking these things? Which is easier: to say to the paralytic, "Your sins are forgiven," or to say, "Get up, take your mat and walk"?'

Then follows the key verse of this passage.

Jesus continued, 'But that you may know that the Son of Man has authority on earth to forgive sins…' – he turned to the paralysed man, 'I tell you, get up, take your mat and go home.' To the amazement of everyone, the man did get up, pick up his mat and walk away.

- Jesus healed because he saw the faith of the friends.
- At first, Jesus did not say 'Get up and walk'. He said, 'Your sins are forgiven.'
- The teachers of the Law – and Jesus – thought that only God could forgive sins. The difference was that Jesus claimed to have authority from God. The teachers of the Law would not believe he had that authority.
- Only God could forgive sin and only God could heal with a word. The fact that Jesus could heal showed he had God's authority. That is why Jesus' words are the key to the passage.
- Jesus did not say 'I have authority'. He said, 'The Son of Man has authority' – clearly meaning he was the Son of Man.

### Mark 8: 31–8, Matthew 16: 21–8. Jesus predicts his death

At Caesarea Philippi, Jesus said the Son of Man must suffer, die and rise again. Peter (who had just said 'You are the Christ') said that this could never happen. Jesus turned on him, saying, 'Get behind me, Satan.' He went on to tell the disciples that each of them must be ready to take up the cross – in other words, to suffer for him. If anyone was ashamed of him, the Son of Man would be ashamed of that person when he came in glory.

**1C** ### Mark 10: 35–45. The request of James and John

Note that Jesus said, 'The Son of Man did not come to be served, but to serve, and to give his life as a ransom for many.'

On James and John see page 48 under Discipleship.

Jesus referred to himself as the Son of Man at the Last Supper (see page 63). He said that the Son of Man would be betrayed, as the **scriptures** said. Even then, the person who betrayed the Son of Man was guilty. Jesus said, 'It would be better for him if he had not been born.' Once again, Jesus used the title of the heavenly being, about whom the prophets had spoken.

## Jesus/Saviour

The name Jesus means Saviour. (See page 13 on Matthew 1: 18–25.) When Christians think of Jesus as Saviour they normally think of him as saving them from sin. In specification option **1C** the following passages have been chosen to symbolize Jesus as Saviour. They describe Jesus saving people from danger, hunger and illness.

**1C** ### Mark 4: 35–41. Jesus calms the storm

As the storm grew fiercer Jesus slept. The disciples woke him – 'Teacher, don't you care if we drown?' Jesus woke and calmed the storm. He said to the disciples, 'Why are you so afraid? Do you still have no faith?' They were filled with awe and said to each other, 'Who is this? Even the wind and the waves obey him!'

**1C** **1D** ### Mark 6: 30–44. The feeding of the five thousand

The people had been listening to Jesus teaching all day. They were hungry and there was no food to be had locally. When the disciples told Jesus that he should send them away he told them to feed them. They protested – 200 denarii would not be enough (a denarius was a day's wage). Jesus had five loaves and two fish. Looking to heaven, he gave thanks and broke them. Everyone was fed – and twelve baskets of broken pieces were left at the end.

**1C** **1D** ### Mark 7: 24–30. The faith of a Syro-Phoenician woman

The Syro-Phoenician woman's daughter had a demon. She heard that Jesus was in the area – which was just outside Galilee. The woman and her daughter were not Jews. Jews believed that they, not the Gentiles, were God's chosen people. Many regarded Gentiles as inferior, even referring to Jews as God's children and Gentiles as dogs. This belief explains Jesus' conversation with the woman.

'First let the children eat all they want,' said Jesus, 'for it is not right to take the children's bread and toss it to their dogs.' The woman was not put off by this. 'Yes, Lord,' she replied, 'but even the dogs under the table eat the children's crumbs.' Jesus was impressed by her faith. 'For such a reply, you may go; the demon has left your daughter.'

Jesus did not regard Gentiles as inferior – but pretended that he did, maybe teasing her, with a twinkle in his eye. He was certainly testing her faith.

## Christ/Messiah/Son of David

- The Jews were waiting for the coming of the Messiah. Messiah is a Hebrew word meaning 'Anointed One'. The Greek word is 'Christ' – so Messiah and Christ mean the same thing.
- Anointing is a **symbol** of dedication to God. Kings, who were descended from King David, were anointed. The Messiah would be a 'Son of David', descended from the great king.
- Prophets had spoken and written about the Messiah. God had promised that he would send the Messiah. People were waiting for the promise to be kept.
- Naturally people wondered if Jesus was the Messiah.
- For Jesus, the title caused a problem. Some people thought the Messiah would be a king in the political sense, a leader of the Jewish nation. For that reason, Jesus at times told people not to speak of him as the Messiah. In the end, he left his followers – and his enemies – in no doubt that he was the Messiah.

> **hints and tips**
>
> Note the words 'Messianic Secret'. The term refers to the way that Jesus told people not to talk about him as the Messiah.

### 1C  *Mark 8: 27–30*  1D  *Matthew 16: 13–20. An incident at Caesarea Philippi*

Jesus asked the disciples who people said he was. They replied that they were saying he was a great religious leader from the past – John the Baptist, Elijah or one of the prophets. (**1D**: Matthew mentions Jeremiah.) 'Who do you say I am?' Jesus then asked them. Peter replied, 'You are the Christ.'

Jesus ordered them to tell no one. Instead he spoke of himself as Son of Man.

**1D**  Matthew's Gospel contains a fuller account.

When Jesus asked, 'Who do you say I am?' Peter answered, 'You are the Christ, the Son of the living God.' Jesus replied, 'This was not revealed to you by man, but by my Father in heaven. And I tell you that you are Peter, and on this rock I will build my **church**, and the gates of Hades will not overcome it. I will give you the keys of the kingdom of heaven; whatever you bind on earth will be bound in heaven, and whatever you loose on earth will be loosed in heaven.'

> **read more**
>
> Look again at the verses which follow these passages, Mark 8: 31–8 and Matthew 16: 21–8.

Jesus is making a play on words since, in Greek, Peter means rock.

### Mark 10: 46–52. Blind Bartimaeus receives his sight

Bartimaeus, a blind man, heard that Jesus was passing. He shouted, 'Jesus, Son of David, have mercy on me!' People told him to be quiet but he kept on shouting. Jesus called for him and asked him what he wanted. Bartimaeus replied, '**Rabbi**, I want to see.' Jesus replied, 'Your faith has healed you.'

**hints and tips**
Note that Bartimaeus welcomed Jesus as the Messiah.

### Mark 11: 1–11. The triumphal entry

By riding into Jerusalem on a donkey Jesus claimed that he was the Messiah, since the prophet Zechariah had written centuries earlier that the Messiah would come to Jerusalem on a donkey. The people who welcomed him got the message – they welcomed him as the Messiah. His enemies got the message too.

Jesus sent two disciples to fetch the donkey, telling them that if anyone asked what they were doing they were to reply, 'The Lord needs it and will send it back here shortly'. As Jesus rode into Jerusalem people spread their clothes and branches from nearby palm trees in front of him. Had they been fore warned they would probably have prepared carpets and garlands of flowers. They shouted 'Hosanna!' (meaning 'save now'), 'Blessed is he who comes in the name of the Lord!', 'Blessed is the coming kingdom of our father David!', 'Hosanna in the highest!'

## What do these titles mean to Christians?

- *Son of God* – Jesus is the Son of God who has always existed. The miracle of the Virgin Birth shows that he is different from ordinary men. In Jesus Christians can see what God is like. His teaching has God's authority. He is the example of a perfect human life. Christians try to imitate Jesus by acting as they think he would in their situation.
- *Son of Man* – Like the Son of Man in the Old Testament, Jesus had the authority of God to forgive sins. Also, his destiny was to suffer and die and to give himself as a ransom for sin.
- *Messiah* – Christians believe that Jesus is the leader promised in the Old Testament, the person who would bring new hope of a great future. They see Jesus as leading people to the **kingdom of God**.
- *Jesus/Saviour* – The name 'Jesus' means 'Saviour'. Christians have faith in Jesus as their Saviour. They believe that through Jesus their sins may be forgiven and that they have hope in eternal life.

**read more**
For what Christians understand by the kingdom of God, see pages 35–41.

## Other events in the life of Jesus  1D

### Luke 4: 1–13. The Temptation

Jesus was led by the Spirit into the desert. There he was tempted. He resisted the temptation, quoting each time from the scriptures. He had fasted (eaten nothing) for 40 days. The devil said to him, 'If you are the Son of God, tell this stone to become bread.' Jesus replied with words of scripture, 'It is written: "Man does not live on bread alone."'

Christians believe that because Jesus is the Son of God he could turn stones into bread, but did not do so because he had come to live a normal human life. He used his divine powers to help others, not to make life easier for himself. Also, when Jesus said, 'Man does not live on bread alone' he did not mean 'live' in the sense of 'exist' but 'live life to the full'.

> The devil took him (presumably in imagination) to a high mountain, from which they could see the whole world. The devil promised to give Jesus all the nations of the world if he would worship him. Jesus refused, saying, 'It is written: "Worship the Lord your God and serve him only."'

Christians believe that Jesus came to bring people to worship God, not the devil. He would not make any agreement with the devil. Good must not compromise with evil.

> The devil took him to the highest point of the temple in Jerusalem. He said, 'If you are the Son of God, throw yourself down. You will come to no harm' – and the devil quoted the scriptures this time: 'He will command his angels concerning you, to guard you carefully.' Jesus answered, 'It says: "Do not put the Lord your God to the test."'

Jesus never used his miraculous power for stunts but only to meet genuine human need.

## Luke 4: 16–30. Jesus rejected at Nazareth

Jesus went to Nazareth, where he had lived as a boy. In the synagogue on the Sabbath he read a passage from the prophet Isaiah about the Spirit giving power – a passage thought by some to refer to the Messiah. After reading, he announced, 'Today this scripture is fulfilled in your hearing.' Everyone was amazed – 'Isn't this Joseph's son?' Jesus said that no doubt they had heard of his **miracles** in Capernaum and expected to see some in his hometown. That was not God's way. Elijah and Elisha the prophets could have helped Jewish people in need in their day – but each chose to help Gentiles. The idea that the person who seemed to be claiming to be the Messiah thought that Gentiles were equal to his own nation made the people angry. They took him to the top of the hill on which the town was built, to throw him down. Jesus walked through them and went away.

### Try these short questions

**a**  What does the name Jesus mean? (1 mark)

**b**  Why did people shout 'Hosanna!' as Jesus rode into Jerusalem? (2 marks)

**c**  Describe an occasion when Jesus healed a Gentile. (4 marks)

## Exam-type questions

**a** Explain what Christians mean when they say that Jesus is the Son of God. (3 marks)

**b** Briefly describe one occasion when Jesus showed he had authority to forgive sin. (2 marks)

**c** 'The Son of Man did not come to be served, but to serve, and to give his life as a ransom for many.' Explain what Christians believe about why God sent Jesus into the world. (3 marks)                                        (SEG, 1998)

### Student's answer

*a Christians mean that Jesus is the Son of God the Father. When he was baptized there was a voice from heaven saying, 'He is my Son.' He existed before he was born on earth. When the angel told Mary and then Joseph that Jesus was going to be born he told them that the Holy Spirit would make Mary pregnant because Jesus was the Son of God, not of Joseph.*

*b Some men brought their friend to Jesus and lowered him on his bed through the roof to get to Jesus. Jesus told the man his sins were forgiven. Some people did not like what Jesus was saying when he healed the man, saying that the fact that he could just say the word and make him well showed that he could forgive sins.*

*c As the quote says, Jesus' death was a ransom, which means that he paid with his life to save people from sin. He died on the cross because he came to save the world.*

### Examiner's comments

**a** This response covers some important points. It states that Christians believe in Jesus as existing before his birth at Bethlehem and explains the idea of the Virgin Birth without actually using the term. There is no indication that as the Son of God he gave an example of what a Christian life should be.                                                    Mark: 2/3

**b** The student has chosen a good example and has shown how forgiveness of sins came into it. Much detail has been left out, but only two marks were available and the student has done enough in a brief answer to gain both marks.                              Mark: 2/2

**c** The student has tried to explain the text given but has not seen the full meaning of the question. The response concentrates only on the death of Jesus as a ransom. There is nothing about the love of God, of the teaching ministry or of his resurrection.              Mark: 1/3

## Examination practice

The high priest asked him, 'Are you the Christ, the Son of the Blessed One?' 'I am,' said Jesus. 'And you will see the Son of Man sitting at the right hand of the Mighty One and coming on the clouds of heaven.'

**a** State two ways in which the High Priest reacted to those words. (2 marks)

**b** Explain the meaning and importance of the words 'the Christ, the Son of the Blessed One'. (4 marks)

**c** Some of those present thought it was blasphemy for Jesus to speak these words. Explain why. (3 marks)                                                              (NEAB, 1999)

# Checklist for revision

| | Understand and know | Need more revision | Do not understand |
|---|---|---|---|
| I know two occasions when Jesus was called the 'Son of God'. | ☐ | ☐ | ☐ |
| I know what is meant by 'Son of Man'. | ☐ | ☐ | ☐ |
| I understand the difference between what people thought the Messiah would be and the sort of Messiah Jesus claimed to be. | ☐ | ☐ | ☐ |
| **1D** I understand why Christians believe that the birth of Jesus was unique. | ☐ | ☐ | ☐ |
| I understand why Jesus matters to Christians today. | ☐ | ☐ | ☐ |

# 3 The suffering and death of Jesus  1A 1B 1C 1D

## Topic summary

Make sure you have the order of events clear in your mind.

- After the Last Supper Jesus went to Gethsemane, on the Mount of Olives, to pray.
- He prayed that he might not have to suffer but ended 'Your will be done'.
- Jesus was betrayed by Judas and arrested. His followers deserted him.
- He was tried by the priests and sentenced to death for **blasphemy**.
- Peter denied that he had ever known Jesus three times.
- Jesus was tried by Pilate, the Roman governor. Under pressure from the priests, Pilate sentenced him to be crucified.
- Jesus was crucified.
- Christians believe that because of the death of Jesus their sins can be forgiven and, when they die, they can be with God in heaven.

## What do I need to know?

- **1A** **1B** Why the crucifixion of Jesus is important to Christians. How and why Christians keep Holy Week.

- **1C** Jesus' example of self-sacrifice and his suffering and death. The central place these events have within Christianity and the Christian belief in life after death.

## The arrest and trials of Jesus

### 1C *Mark 14: 32–52. Gethsemane and Jesus' arrest*

After the Last Supper Jesus went with his **disciples** to a place called Gethsemane on the Mount of Olives, just outside Jerusalem. He told his disciples to sit while he prayed: three of them, Peter, James and John, he took to be nearer him. As Jesus prayed, he was very distressed. He prayed, 'Abba, Father, everything is possible for you. Take this cup from me. Yet not what I will, but what you will.'

> **did you know?**
> 'Abba' is **Aramaic** for 'Daddy', the natural way for children to address their father.

When Jesus prayed 'Take this cup from me', he was asking to be spared the suffering. (Remember what he said to James and John, Mark 10: 35–45 – see page 17.) But he was obedient to the Father – God's will would be done.

Three times Jesus went back to the disciples and each time found them asleep. The third time a band of soldiers led by Judas came to arrest Jesus. As he had arranged with the soldiers, Judas greeted Jesus with a kiss then they arrested him. One disciple drew his sword to defend Jesus and cut off the ear of the High Priest's servant. Jesus asked why they were ambushing him as though he was a dangerous rebel – they could have arrested him in the temple while he was teaching there. His followers deserted him and ran away – among them a young man who, when they grabbed what he was wearing, ran off naked. (There is a tradition that this was Mark himself, though there is no evidence to prove it.)

## 1D Luke 22: 39–53. Jesus prays on the Mount of Olives, then is arrested

After the Last Supper Jesus went with his disciples to the Mount of Olives, just outside Jerusalem. He told his disciples to pray. He went a little way from them and prayed: 'Father, if you are willing, take this cup from me; yet not my will, but yours be done.' Jesus felt the normal human fear of suffering. He was in agony as he prayed. He prayed so intensely that his sweat was like drops of blood falling on the ground. An angel from heaven appeared to him to strengthen him.

*Jesus suffered greatly as he prayed in Gethsemane – his **prayer** is known as 'The Agony in the Garden'.*

When Jesus prayed 'Take this cup from me', he was asking to be spared the suffering. But he was obedient to the Father – God's will would be done.

When Jesus went back to the disciples he found them asleep. The third time a crowd led by Judas came to arrest Jesus. Judas greeted Jesus with a kiss then they arrested him. One disciple drew his sword to defend Jesus and cut off the ear of the High Priest's servant. Jesus asked why they were ambushing him as though he was a dangerous rebel – they could have arrested him in the temple while he was teaching there.

## 1C   1D   Mark 14: 53–65. Before the Sanhedrin

The members of the Council were looking for reasons to condemn Jesus but they could not find anything on which two witnesses agreed. Even when they reported that Jesus had said he would destroy the temple and in three days would build another not made with hands, the witnesses did not agree.

Jesus remained silent until the High Priest challenged him directly, 'Are you the Christ, the Son of the Blessed One?' Jesus answered, 'I am, and you will see the Son of Man sitting at the right hand of the Mighty One and coming on the clouds of heaven.'

That was enough. Jesus had claimed to be the Son of God. Since they believed there was only one God, Jesus could not be the Son of God. He had used God's name wrongly, he had made himself equal with God. In other words, Jesus was guilty of blasphemy. The punishment was death.

The High Priest tore his robe – a symbol that someone was guilty of blasphemy. All agreed that they did not need other witnesses. Everyone had heard what Jesus had said. Some spat at him, the guards beat him. To make fun of the idea that he was the Son of God, they blindfolded him, struck him with their fists and told him to say who had struck him. If he was the Son of God and knew everything, they reckoned he should have been able to tell.

### 1C *Mark 15: 1–20. The Roman trial and the mocking*

The priests could state that Jesus was guilty of blasphemy and, under Jewish Law, should be sentenced to death. They could not order the sentence to be carried out. They took Jesus to Pilate, the Roman governor. 'Are you the king of the Jews?' asked Pilate, to which Jesus replied, 'Yes, it is as you say.' The priests made accusations against him. To Pilate's amazement, Jesus did not reply.

There was a custom that every year at Passover a prisoner would be released. Pilate offered the people a choice – Jesus or Barabbas, a notorious criminal.

Pilate must have thought that Barabbas was so bad a criminal that the crowd would choose Jesus. They shouted for Barabbas to be released and Jesus to be crucified. Pilate gave in. He had Jesus flogged and sentenced him to be crucified.

The soldiers made fun of Jesus, King of the Jews. They dressed him as a king, in a purple robe (purple was the colour for royalty). They made a crown of thorns to go on his head with big, viciously painful thorns. They bowed before him with mock homage, 'Hail, King of the Jews.' Then they dressed him again in his own clothes and sent him to be crucified.

read more

Mark 14: 66–72, Luke 22: 54–62. Peter denies knowing Jesus

See under Discipleship, page 47

## The trials of Jesus were not proper trials

The trial before the Council was unfair for these reasons.

- It took place at night, immediately after Jesus was arrested. Jesus had no chance to prepare a proper defence.
- The trial should have begun with Jesus being charged with an offence. Instead, his opponents were looking for some charge to bring against him.
- A trial judge should be unbiased. At Jesus' trial the High Priest was against Jesus.
- Witnesses at a trial had to agree – they did not at Jesus' trial.

The trial before Pilate was unfair for these reasons.

- There was no time for Jesus to arrange a proper defence, with someone to represent him, even though he faced a possible death sentence.
- At a proper trial the judge does not offer a choice of prisoners to be released.
- In a proper trial the judge is not influenced by the shouting of a crowd.
- Pilate sentenced Jesus to be flogged and crucified without making clear why he was sentencing him. Indeed, Pilate seemed to think Jesus was innocent. The words of the accusation nailed to the cross, 'The King of the Jews', did not explain what the offence was.

## The crucifixion and burial of Jesus

### 1C 1D *Mark 15: 21–41. The Crucifixion*

Simon of Cyrene, a passer-by, was forced to help Jesus carry the cross to Golgotha, where Jesus was crucified. Jesus refused wine mixed with myrrh, offered to deaden his pain. Above his cross were written the words, 'The King of the Jews', showing why Jesus was being executed. Two robbers were crucified at the same time, one on each side of Jesus.

Passers-by made fun of Jesus. 'You who are going to destroy the temple and build it in three days, come down from the cross and save yourself!' The chief priests and teachers of the Law said, 'He saved others, but he can't save himself! Let this Christ, this King of Israel, come down now from the cross, that we may see and believe.' If Jesus had come down from the cross unharmed they would believe he was the **Messiah**. Those being crucified with him joined in the mocking.

The land was in darkness from midday to mid-afternoon. Jesus called out in a loud voice, *'Eloi, Eloi, lama sabachthani?'* Hebrew words meaning, 'My God, my God, why have you forsaken me?' Some bystanders deliberately pretended to think that Jesus was calling on Elijah (a great prophet who had died over 800 years earlier) to help him.

Almost immediately after that, when Jesus died, the curtain of the temple split in half. The centurion, the Roman officer in charge of the crucifixion, when he saw and heard everything, said, 'Surely this man was the Son of God!' (See page 15)

**1D** Luke 23: 32–43 gives further information about the crucifixion.

- As Jesus was nailed to the cross he prayed, 'Father, forgive them, for they do not know what they are doing.'

- One of the criminals being crucified with him joined in the mockery – 'Aren't you the Christ? Save yourself and us!' The other criminal rebuked him. 'Don't you fear God,' he said, 'since you are under the same sentence? We are punished justly, for we are getting what our deeds deserve. But this man has done nothing wrong.' Then he said, 'Jesus, remember me when you come into your kingdom.' Jesus answered him, 'I tell you the truth, today you will be with me in paradise.'

## 1C Mark 15: 42–47. *The burial of Jesus*

Joseph of Arimathaea, a member of the Jewish Council who was a follower of Jesus, asked Pilate for Jesus' body. He wrapped it in linen cloth and placed it in a tomb cut into rock. He sealed the tomb with a large stone. Mary Magdalene and other women saw where Jesus was buried. They could not complete the burial **rites** since it was almost sunset, the beginning of the Sabbath. They had to wait until the Sabbath was over.

# Why is the suffering and death of Jesus important to Christians?

The trials of Jesus were not conducted properly. On the face of it, Jesus was the helpless victim of ruthless enemies. However, Christians see the death of Jesus as being part of God's plan to save the human race. Jesus could have avoided the crucifixion – but chose not to do so.

- Jesus knew he was going to be put to death. He told his disciples that he would die and rise again. 'Jesus began to teach his disciples that the Son of Man must suffer many things and be rejected by the elders, chief priests and teachers of the Law, and that he must be killed and after three days rise again.' (Mark 8: 31, see page 17) The disciples did not realize what he was talking about until after the **resurrection**.

- Jesus went deliberately towards his death. He knew that by riding into Jerusalem on a donkey he was claiming to be the Messiah – and that would provoke his enemies to get rid of him. After the Last Supper he went to Gethsemane, even though he knew that Judas had arranged for him to be arrested there. He did not try to defend himself in his trials.

Christians think of the death of Jesus as a wonderful mystery which human beings cannot fully understand. They think of his death in a number of different ways, each showing something of that mystery.

- Jesus once spoke of his death as a ransom (Mark 10: 45). His death was a punishment for human sin. Human beings may enter heaven, even though they have sinned, since Jesus has paid the penalty instead of them.
- Jesus' death was the completion of God's plan to save the human race. He prepared for the coming of Jesus through prophets who taught that one day the Messiah would come.
- In the Old Testament people offered **sacrifices** every year to show their sorrow for their sins and to ask forgiveness. Jesus' death is the perfect sacrifice, the offering of a perfect life, something which the offerings of animals or crops could not be. Other offerings were repeated year by year; his sacrifice need never be repeated. The power of his goodness is enough to save all people of every race and every century.
- Jesus' death **atones** for sin – Jesus bridges the gap between God and the human race and reconciles human beings with the Father.
- The crucifixion is a sign of God's love. 'God so loved the world that he gave his one and only Son, that whoever believes in him shall not perish but have eternal life.' (John 3: 16)

Christians do not believe that, because Jesus died on the cross, everyone's sins are automatically forgiven. Each individual must **repent**, turn to Jesus and accept him as Saviour. They believe that those who accept Jesus as their Saviour and who follow him may enter God's kingdom with their sins forgiven.

Baptism is a way of sharing in the forgiveness made available through the sacrifice of Jesus. Paul writes of baptism as dying to sin and rising with Christ.

## Try these short questions

**a** Soldiers crucified Jesus. State two other things the soldiers did or said at his crucifixion. (2 marks)

**b** As Jesus died on the cross, he cried out, '*Eloi, Eloi, lama sabachthani?*' What do these words mean? (2 marks)                    (NEAB, 2000)

## Exam-type questions

**a** Describe in detail the Roman trial of Jesus before Pilate (do not include the mocking of Jesus by the Roman soldiers). (8 marks)

**b** Explain the meaning and importance of the death of Jesus for Christians today. (5 marks)

(NEAB, 2001)

### Student's answer

*a Jesus was brought to Pilate to be given a trial. Pilate did not know why Jesus had been arrested or what he had done wrong. He offered the people a choice – he would release either Jesus or a criminal called Barabbas. The crowd chose Barabbas so Pilate had Jesus whipped and crucified.*

*b Jesus' death was a sacrifice. He died to take away the sins of the world. It was all part of God's plan because Jesus was the Messiah sent from God. Jesus died so that everyone could go to heaven when they die.*

### Examiner's comments

**a** This is a typical answer which looks quite good until one sees just how much has been left out. The student has omitted the point that Jesus was brought to Pilate by the priests who were making accusations against him. Pilate's opening question, 'Are you the king of the Jews?' shows what the accusations were about; the student should have included it. Jesus' reply, 'Yes, it is as you say,' and the point that he made no other answer to the accusations should also have been mentioned. Other points omitted are that the offer to release a prisoner was a Passover custom and that the crowd were shouting that they wanted Jesus crucified.                    Mark: 3/8

**b** A number of points are made – the ideas of sacrifice, God's plan and the possibility of humans entering heaven are all mentioned, though none has been fully explained. The examiner would not expect every possible idea to be explained in full, but would want some of the ideas developed. For instance, the student should have said what a sacrifice is and in what sense Jesus' death was a sacrifice.                    Mark: 3/5

## Examination practice

**a** Describe the events that took place on the Mount of Olives, in Gethsemane, on the night before Jesus' crucifixion. (4 marks)

**b** **1D** How could Christians show in their behaviour and attitudes that they understand the following words said by Jesus on the cross: 'Father, forgive them, for they do not know what they are doing'? (3 marks) (SEG, 1998)

## Checklist for revision

|  | Understand and know | Need more revision | Do not understand |
|---|---|---|---|
| I know the order in which the events described in this section happened. | ☐ | ☐ | ☐ |
| I can describe the trials of Jesus and say why they were not proper trials. | ☐ | ☐ | ☐ |
| I understand why the death of Jesus is important to Christians. | ☐ | ☐ | ☐ |

# 4 Resurrection and life after death  `1A 1B 1C 1D`

## Topic summary

- Jesus had been crucified and buried. Everyone accepted that he was dead.
- The Gospels record that on the first day of the week, two days after the crucifixion, the tomb was empty.
- Jesus was seen by followers after the resurrection.
- When first they discovered the empty tomb the **disciples** were puzzled. When they saw Jesus they were convinced that he had risen.
- To Christians, the resurrection is the most important event in history. They believe that, because Jesus died and then rose again, eternal life is possible for those who follow him.

## What do I need to know?

- The basic evidence for belief in the resurrection – the empty tomb and the witnesses who saw the risen Jesus.
- Set Bible passages.
    - `1C`  Mark 12: 18–27; Mark 16: 1–20
    - `1D`  Matthew 28: 1–15; Mark 16: 1–8; Luke 24: 1–53
- The meaning for Christians of the resurrection of Jesus.
- `1A`  `1B`  `1D`  The meaning for Christians of the ascension of Jesus.
- The importance of Easter and how different denominations celebrate it.

**read more**

For Mark 16: 16–18, see Section 7, page 49

## What the Gospels say: The empty tomb

All the **Gospel** writers tell how women went to the tomb early.

### `1C`  `1D`  *Mark 16: 1–8*

Mary Magdalene and two other women went to the tomb to anoint Jesus' body, wondering who would roll the stone aside for them. They found the stone rolled away and the body gone. They saw a young man in a white robe and they were afraid. The young man said, 'Don't be alarmed. You are looking for Jesus the Nazarene, who was crucified. He has risen! He is not here. See the place where they laid him.' They had to tell the disciples, especially Peter, that they would see Jesus in Galilee. The women ran away, afraid.

**hints and tips**

In **1C** you may be asked what the young man said to the women – make sure you know!

### `1D`  *Luke 24: 1–12*

The women found the stone rolled away and the body gone. Two men in bright clothes told them Jesus had risen, as he had said he would. The women told the disciples, who did not believe them.

**1D** *Matthew 28: 1–15*

There was an earthquake. An angel came and rolled back the stone. The guards were terrified. The angel told the women that Jesus had risen. As they went away, Jesus met them. When the guards reported what had happened they were bribed to keep quiet.

## What the Gospels say: People saw Jesus alive  1C  1D

Only when Jesus' followers actually saw him did they believe that he had risen. They could not believe it until they had seen him for themselves.

- *Mark* lists the people to whom Jesus appeared. They told others, but no one would believe it. When he met the disciples for the last time he told them, 'Go into all the world and preach the good news to all **creation**.' (Mark 16: 9–20)

**1D** Read about the walk to Emmaus (Luke 24: 13–35)

## The risen Jesus

- In one sense, Jesus' body was the same after the resurrection as before. He could be recognized. His wounds were clearly visible.
- In another way, he was different, no longer limited by laws of nature. Jesus could come and go without restriction, even through closed doors.

**hints and tips**

Note in Luke 24 what Jesus said to the disciples when he appeared to them in Jerusalem.

## Why the resurrection is important to Christians

- It is a sign that Jesus is God the Son. His power over sin and evil is so great that death and hell could not control him.
- They believe it shows there is life after death. Jesus died on the Friday. He rose on the Sunday. That means he did not cease to exist when he died. Christians believe that when they die they will not cease to exist. They believe there will be life in heaven for those who love and serve Jesus.
- They believe that Jesus is present with Christians today. After the resurrection he told his disciples, 'I am with you always, to the very end of the age.'

Some Christians find it hard to accept that Jesus rose physically. That does not mean that they do not believe in the resurrection; though Jesus died on the cross, he is alive.

**did you know?**

Sunday is the Christian holy day because it is the day of the resurrection. See pages 55–58.

## The ascension of Jesus

Mark and Luke both describe how Jesus ascended to heaven. His followers saw him go up until a cloud hid him from sight. Both stress that Jesus went to heaven – in Mark's words, 'took his seat at the right hand of God.' The response of Jesus' followers was positive. They returned to Jerusalem joyfully. They set about their mission of spreading the Gospel. The ascension is important to Christians for several reasons.

- Jesus' earthly ministry had a triumphant ending.
- Jesus returned to reign in glory, as he had done before his birth at Bethlehem.
- At his birth Jesus took a human nature. He retained his human nature when he entered heaven. Christians believe he keeps for ever both his divine and his human nature.

- Jesus promised that he would prepare a place in heaven for his followers.
- Jesus in heaven eternally prays for the human race, presenting to the Father his sacrifice of himself on the cross. Christians link their prayers to his **prayer** – they use words such as 'through Jesus Christ our Lord'.

# Life after death

**1C** *Mark 12: 18–27. Marriage at the resurrection*

The Sadducees did not believe in life after death. They tried to make the idea seem ridiculous. They described a possible situation and asked Jesus his opinion.

See page 7 on the Sadducees.

> There were seven brothers. The eldest married a woman and then died, leaving her childless. The second took her as his wife and also died childless. In the same way, each married her and then died. Last of all, the woman died. Whose wife would she be in heaven?

Jesus replied that heaven was not like that. People would not marry, as in life on earth. They would be like angels. He went on to challenge the Sadducees about life after death. They spent a great deal of time studying the Law. They would not have liked it when Jesus told them that they did not know the scriptures if they did not believe in life after death. Jesus pointed out that in the Law God said to Moses, 'I am the God of Abraham, Isaac and Jacob.' They had all been dead for centuries. If God said, 'I am their God' then they still existed, after death.

# What Christians believe about life after death

- Christians believe that their souls never cease to exist. Even when the body dies, the **soul** lives on.
- There will be a judgement. Christians do not believe that all go to heaven. Sometimes it seems that there is a judgement immediately after death (note the parable of the rich man and Lazarus, Luke 16: 19–31). Sometimes it appears that the judgement will be at the end of the world (Matthew 25: 31–46).
- There are two important points about Christian belief in a judgement.
  1 The judgement is based on people's relationships with God and neighbour. The two great **commandments** are 'Love God' and 'Love your neighbour'.
  2 There is always room for repentance. Those who **repent**, however late in life, may have God's forgiveness.
- The disciples saw Jesus go up as he ascended. Christians do not take that to mean that he kept going until he reached a place called heaven. Heaven is not a place that could be marked on the map. It is a state of the soul, rather like a state of mind. Heaven is being with God. Hell is being separated from God.
- When Christians say they believe in the resurrection of the body, they do not mean that the physical body is restored exactly as it was. It means that they will be individuals still, recognizable as themselves.
- Eternal life is what it says. It is never ending. It is more than just existing; it is living the risen life to the full.

**beware**

Do not mention *reincarnation!* Christians do not believe in reincarnation (which means returning to live on earth in a different form).

# Christian death rites  1A  1C

## *Funerals*

Christian death **rites** are centred on belief in life after death. The main emphasis is on a **faith** and hope in the power of the death and resurrection of Jesus. Jesus died to take away the sins of the world. Christians who have followed Jesus and have accepted him as Saviour will be welcomed to eternal life with God.

Obviously, many of those attending a funeral service are grieving over the loss of a loved one. Bereavement is a hard time. Not only is there the sadness caused by the loved one's death, the lives of those closest to the deceased may never be the same again. However, the service is not intended to be mournful. It is the celebration of the life which has ended. It is full of hope that there is life in heaven after death.

The usual pattern of a funeral service is as follows.

- The minister leads the coffin and the close mourners into the **church** or chapel.
- There is a Bible reading which focuses on the Christian hope of eternal life.
- There is usually a eulogy (a tribute to the deceased) including an account of their life and particular things for which they will be remembered.
- There are prayers of thanksgiving for the dead person's life.
- The **congregation** pray for the soul of the deceased. They also pray for the bereaved, that God will help and comfort them.
- The body is taken for burial or cremation.

## *Roman Catholic Requiem Mass*

A Roman Catholic funeral is usually a Eucharist. It is known as a Requiem Mass because requiem, meaning rest, is, in the Latin funeral Mass, the first word of the opening sentence, 'Eternal rest grant to them O Lord.'

- Sometimes the coffin is brought to the church the previous evening. Otherwise the procession of the hearse followed by the mourners arrives at the beginning of the Mass. The priest sprinkles the coffin with holy water and leads the procession into the church.
- The readings at the Mass concentrate on the Christian belief in life after death through the power of the death and resurrection of Jesus. The prayers at the Mass, especially the Eucharistic Prayer, emphasize the Christian hope of eternal life.
- In the homily the preacher pays tribute to the deceased and speaks of the hope of heaven which is central to the Christian faith.
- The congregation recall their belief in God as a loving Father. They pray for the deceased and for those who mourn.
- The funeral is followed by burial or cremation.

## Try these short questions

**a** The Sadducees told Jesus about a woman who married seven brothers. What question did the Sadducees then ask Jesus? (2 marks)

**b** How did Jesus answer the Sadducees? (3 marks)

**c** Explain how a belief in resurrection gives hope to Christians. (2 marks)

## Exam-type questions

Explain the role of Mary Magdalene and the other women in the resurrection story. (3 marks)

(SEG, 1998)

### Student's answer

*The women came to the grave of Jesus to finish burying him. They found the stone had been rolled away. Two angels in bright clothes appeared. The women were frightened but the angels told them not to be afraid because Jesus had risen. The women went to tell the disciples but they did not believe it.*

### Examiner's comments

The question is about the women, not the men in white. This is a good account of what the Gospel says. The question goes a little deeper than that. It asks about their *role*. The women were the first witnesses of the empty tomb, the first to be told that Jesus had risen. The belief that the tomb was empty and the body had gone is very important to Christians. Mark: 2/3

## Examination practice

**a** State what the young man/two men/angel at the tomb told the women. (2 marks)

**b** 'The empty tomb is the most important **symbol** of the Christian faith.' Do you agree? Give reasons for your answer, showing you have thought about more than one point of view. (5 marks) (NEAB, 2000)

## Checklist for revision

| | Understand and know | Need more revision | Do not understand |
|---|:---:|:---:|:---:|
| I know what Christians mean by the resurrection of Jesus. | ☐ | ☐ | ☐ |
| I can explain why the resurrection of Jesus is important to Christians. | ☐ | ☐ | ☐ |
| 1C  1D  I can describe two appearances of Jesus after the resurrection. | ☐ | ☐ | ☐ |
| I know what Christians believe about life after death. | ☐ | ☐ | ☐ |
| I can describe and understand a Christian death rite. | ☐ | ☐ | ☐ |

# 5 The kingdom of God

## Topic summary

- The **kingdom of God** is a central part of Jesus' teaching.
- The kingdom exists wherever God is accepted as king. Jesus taught his followers to think about the kingdom in two ways.
  1. The kingdom exists on earth wherever individuals personally accept God's rule and commit themselves to worshipping and serving him.
  2. The kingdom exists in heaven where God reigns in glory.
- Christians today see themselves as building up the kingdom of God on earth whilst believing that after death they may enter the kingdom in heaven.

## What do I need to know?

- The ways in which Jesus spoke about the kingdom, on earth and in heaven.
- The Bible passages in your option.
  - **1C** Mark 1: 14–15; Mark 4: 1–34; Mark 10: 13–16, 17–27; Matthew 12: 28–34
  - **1D** Matthew 6: 5–15; Matthew 13: 1–46; Matthew 25: 14–46; Mark 6: 30–44
  - **2B** Matthew 13; Mark 12: 28–31
- How Christians today think about the kingdom.

## What did Jesus mean by the kingdom?

The kingdom of God is central to the teaching of Jesus.

**1C** Note that the first point Jesus makes in his teaching is about the kingdom. After the opening verses describing the baptism of Jesus and his time in the wilderness, Mark continues: 'After John was put in prison, Jesus went into Galilee, proclaiming the good news of God. "The time has come," he said. "The kingdom of God is near. Repent and believe the good news!"' (Mark 1: 14–15)

**hints and tips**

Jesus sometimes spoke of the kingdom on earth, sometimes the kingdom in heaven. Always make clear which you are describing.

The kingdom of God on earth exists wherever God is accepted as king. In particular, the kingdom is in the hearts of people who love and serve him.

- The kingdom grows as more people accept God's kingship.
- Those people who are members of the kingdom live in society like everyone else. When people die they will face the **Last Judgement**. Those who have been members of the kingdom on earth will enter heaven.

The kingdom of God in heaven is where God reigns, among the angels and all those people who have been received into heaven. In heaven, God's reign is accepted by all.

# Jesus' teaching about the kingdom

### 1D *Matthew 6: 5–15. The Lord's Prayer*

'Your kingdom come, your will be done on earth as it is in heaven.' The words link the two aspects of the kingdom. God's will is done in heaven. Christians pray that in the same way God's will may be done on earth – that his kingship may be accepted.

### 1C 2B *Mark 12: 28–34. The great commandments*

The most important laws in God's kingdom are not like human laws. Human laws say what must or must not be done and sets punishments for those who break the law. The great **commandments** are about the basic attitude of a person's heart.

- Love the Lord your God with all your heart and with all your **soul** and with all your mind and with all your strength.
- Love your neighbour as yourself.

A teacher of the Law had asked Jesus, 'Of all the commandments, which is the most important?' When he heard Jesus' reply he told Jesus he agreed that there were no other commandments as important as these.

Note what Jesus said to the teacher: 'You are not far from the kingdom of God.' He clearly believed that it was essential to have the right state of mind, loving God and loving your neighbour.

### 1C *Mark 10: 13–16. Jesus and the children*

When the children were brought to Jesus the disciples wanted to turn them away. When Jesus saw what was happening he was very annoyed. He said, 'Let the little children come to me, and do not hinder them, for the kingdom of God belongs to such as these. I tell you the truth, anyone who does not receive the kingdom of God like a little child will never enter it.' He took the children in his arms and blessed them.

Jesus meant that people must be trusting and innocent to enter the kingdom. They must have **faith** in God just as young children trust their fathers.

### 1C *Mark 10: 17–27. The rich young ruler*

The rich young ruler asked Jesus what he had to do to gain eternal life. Jesus told him he must obey the commandments, such as 'Do not murder, do not commit **adultery**, do not steal, do not give false **testimony**, do not defraud, honour your father and mother.' The man replied that he had kept them since his youth. Jesus looked at him and, we are told, loved him – so what Jesus said next was not meant to be unkind or to catch him out. He told him that he should give all his possessions to the poor and follow Jesus. The young man could not do that. He went away, obviously upset.

Jesus said it was very hard for the rich to enter the kingdom. It was easier for a camel to go through the eye of a needle than for a rich man to enter the kingdom of God. By this he meant that it was virtually impossible. (Some people have said that there was a tiny gate into Jerusalem called 'Eye of a needle' through which a camel could only go with difficulty – but there is no evidence at all that such a gate ever existed!)

> The disciples asked, 'Then who can be saved?' They were puzzled. If rich, important people will not be accepted, then who will? Jesus tells them that what seems impossible to human beings is not impossible with God.

Jesus meant that the standards of the kingdom are not those of the everyday world – money, status, image. The standards are Christian standards – love of God and love of your neighbour.

## Matthew 13: 1–23, Mark 4: 1–20. The parable of the sower

The **parable** of the sower is an allegory. That means that each feature in the parable has a symbolic meaning.

> When the sower sowed seed, some fell by the wayside and the birds ate it. Some fell on rocky ground, where there was little soil; it grew quickly but in the heat of the sun it withered because it had no moisture or depth of soil. Some fell among thorns which choked it and so prevented growth. Some fell on good soil and grew well, bearing a good crop. Jesus ended with the puzzling statement, 'He who has ears to hear, let him hear.'

On the face of it, that is a simple description of what would have been an everyday event. The disciples realized that there was a deeper meaning and asked Jesus about it. Jesus told them that the parable would make little sense to those who heard it – unless they realized it was about the kingdom.

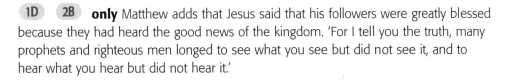

**1D** **2B** **only** Matthew adds that Jesus said that his followers were greatly blessed because they had heard the good news of the kingdom. 'For I tell you the truth, many prophets and righteous men longed to see what you see but did not see it, and to hear what you hear but did not hear it.'

Jesus explained that the different places where seed fell represented different ways in which people respond to the **Gospel** of the kingdom.

- The seed which fell by the wayside represents people who do not even listen to the Gospel.
- The seed which fell on rocky ground represents people who are full of enthusiasm at first but who just as quickly lose interest.
- The seed which fell among thorns represents people who are distracted by problems and other interests.
- The seed which fell on good soil represents people who not only accept the Gospel but pass on the good news to others.

# Other parables of the kingdom

Most of the parables are not allegories. Each parable makes a simple clear point.

### 1C Mark 4: 21–2. The lamp on a stand

Jesus asked, 'Do you bring in a lamp to put it under a bowl or a bed? Instead, don't you put it on its stand?' The Gospel, the good news of the kingdom, is not to be hidden – it is to be made known to everyone.

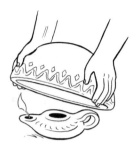

### 1C Mark 4: 26–9. The parable of the growing seed

The kingdom of God is similar to when a man sows seed and the seed grows, unnoticed, first the stalk, then the ear, then the fully ripened grain. At last the ripened grain is harvested. The kingdom grows steadily, unnoticed, until, in time, those who have accepted God's kingship are welcomed into heaven.

### 1D 2B Matthew 13: 24–30, 36–43. The parable of the wheat and the weeds

This parable is sometimes called 'The parable of the weeds'.

> A man sows wheat in his field. An enemy secretly sows weeds among the wheat. The owner tells his servants not to pull up the weeds, in case they pull up the wheat as well. When the harvest is ready, then the weeds will be burned while the wheat is stored in the barn.

Jesus explained that the owner is God and the enemy is the devil. Those who accept God as king and those who do not live together in the world. Christians should not be discouraged by evil in the world. At the Last Judgement those who serve God will be received into the kingdom and the others rejected.

### 1C Mark 4: 30–2 1D 2B Matthew 13: 31–2. The parable of the mustard seed

Jesus said the mustard seed was the smallest of seeds, yet grew to a large tree so that birds could sit on the branches. The kingdom had very small beginnings – Jesus and his band of followers – but would grow to be great. The birds in the branches may symbolize people of all nations entering the kingdom.

### 1D 2B Matthew 13: 33. The parable of the yeast

The kingdom is an influence in the world, reaching everywhere.

### 1D 2B Matthew 13: 44–6. The parable of the treasure hidden in a field and the parable of the pearl of great value

A man who realizes the value of the field or of the pearl gives everything to get it. In the same way, a person who realizes how important it is to enter the kingdom will sacrifice everything to do so.

**1D** **2B** *Matthew 13: 47–50. The parable of the net*

All sorts of fish were in the net when it was brought ashore. The fishermen saved the good fish in baskets, but threw the bad away. At the Last Judgement angels will separate the wicked from the righteous. Only the righteous will enter the kingdom.

**1D** **2B** *Matthew 25: 14–46. The parables of the talents (three servants) and the sheep and the goats*

See page 146. Since the parable of the sheep and the goats is also in option **2A** you will need to know it whatever options you are studying – but do not use it when writing about Mark's Gospel.

## The kingdom today

Christians say the Lord's Prayer daily. When they do so, they can understand in terms either of this life or life in heaven. Christians believe in the kingdom in both senses and both are important.

### The kingdom in heaven

Christians believe that everyone will be judged. Some will be accepted into the kingdom. Those who have faith in Jesus and follow his teachings have a real hope of eternal life. Heaven is the state of being with God. Christians believe that their loved ones who have accepted God as king are welcomed into heaven. They hope and pray that when their lives end they will enter heaven through their faith in Jesus Christ as Saviour and king.

### The kingdom on earth

Christians pray for the growth of the kingdom on earth and try to make it grow.

- They pray that people of every race and nationality may come to know and love Jesus.
- They see **worship** as a way of showing their love of God. Worship is a form of witness – showing that God is important in their lives.
- Christians try to show their love of their neighbour in practical ways. As individuals they have a duty to give help and support to people who need it. There are many agencies through which Christians can help people in need in any part of world.
- Christians also try to bring others into the kingdom. They may encourage other people to worship with them. They may show what their faith means simply by the way they live.

### The kingdom and the Church

Christians use the word '**church**' in a number of different ways.

- A building where people worship.
- One of the denominations, for example, Roman Catholic, Methodist.
- All Christian people who accept God as king. This definition is very close to being a definition of the kingdom of God.

**hints and tips**

Many students find these parables difficult. For each parable, you must understand

- the parable itself
- what it says about the kingdom.

## Try these short questions

**a** Sometimes Jesus spoke about the kingdom on earth, sometimes about the kingdom in heaven. How was he thinking of the kingdom in the following parables?

- The sower (3 marks)
- The wheat and the weeds (3 marks)
- The yeast (2 marks)
- The pearl of great value. (3 marks)

**b** Read these two sayings. To whom did Jesus say them and why?

- 'You are not far from the kingdom of God.' (3 marks)
- 'Let the little children come to me.' (3 marks)

## Exam-type questions

Explain how, according to Mark, Jesus showed people that their words and actions were connected with the kingdom of God. You may include in your answer the parables and sayings of the kingdom, Jesus' teaching about entry into the kingdom, Jesus' words to the lawyer on the great commandments. (8 marks)                                                                    (NEAB, 1997)

### Student's answer

*Jesus said that if a person loved God and loved his neighbour he could enter the kingdom. He told a lawyer that these were the two great commandments. The lawyer agreed. Jesus told him, 'You are not far from the kingdom of God.'*

*Another time he said that you had to be like a child to enter the kingdom. He meant that you had to trust God like a child trusts his father. You have to show you love God and trust him by doing things that will please him.*

*Jesus talked about the kingdom in parables. He said that if someone realized how important the kingdom was they would do everything they could to be part of it. I suppose that means they would really try to show love of God and of their neighbours in a practical way. That way they will perhaps show other people how they should live, so those people become part of the kingdom as well.*

### Examiner's comments

The student has paid attention to the hints given by the examiner and has written about each of the passages mentioned. The material has been arranged quite well. The two great commandments have been put first to show what a person must do to enter the kingdom. It would have been better if there had been some explanation of the way in which loving God and your neighbour affected the way a person lives. The part about being like a child to enter the kingdom is accurately described and briefly explained.

In the part about the teaching in the parables, the student has explained quite well the teaching of two parables. Unfortunately, there is nothing to say which parables. The examiner would realize that the student knew which parable was which, since the explanations are clear. Even so, credit cannot be given for what is not there. A little care would gain a higher mark.                    Mark: 5/8

## Examination practice

**a** What can Christians learn about the kingdom of God from the parable of the weeds? (3 marks)

**b** What can Christians learn about the kingdom of God from the parable of the mustard seed? (3 marks)                                                   (Based on NEAB, 1999)

**c** Show how Christians today could help to make God's kingdom grow. (5 marks)     (SEG, 1998)

## Checklist for revision

| | Understand and know | Need more revision | Do not understand |
|---|:---:|:---:|:---:|
| I understand what 'kingdom of God' means. | ☐ | ☐ | ☐ |
| I can tell each of these parables in my own words and can say what each means. | | | |
| ● The sower | ☐ | ☐ | ☐ |
| ● The wheat and the weeds | ☐ | ☐ | ☐ |
| ● The mustard seed | ☐ | ☐ | ☐ |
| ● The yeast | ☐ | ☐ | ☐ |
| ● The pearl of great value | ☐ | ☐ | ☐ |
| ● The treasure in the field | ☐ | ☐ | ☐ |
| ● The net. | ☐ | ☐ | ☐ |
| I know and understand why Jesus said a person must be like a child to enter the kingdom. | ☐ | ☐ | ☐ |
| I can describe the meeting of Jesus and the rich young ruler. | ☐ | ☐ | ☐ |
| I know the two great commandments and why Jesus said they were important. | ☐ | ☐ | ☐ |

# 6 Jesus' teaching on faith and prayer

1C 1D

## Topic summary

- Jesus performed many **miracles** during his ministry.
- Many of the miracles were performed because people had faith. Jesus stressed the importance of faith and prayer.
- Jesus' miracles showed that he had power over nature, evil spirits, disease and death. His followers were convinced that his power could only have come from God.
- Jesus offered healing of mind and spirit as well as of body. He not only healed a person's bodily illness, he also gave forgiveness for their sins.

## What do I need to know?

- The miracles of Jesus which are part of your specification.
    - **1C** Mark 5: 21–43; Mark 9: 14–29
    - **1D** Mark 4: 35–41; Mark 5: 21–43; Mark 7: 24–30; Matthew 14: 22–33; Luke 7: 1–10; Luke 17: 11–19
- The importance of faith in each miracle.
- How faith is important to Christians today.

## The miracles of Jesus

### Mark 5: 21–4, 35–43. Jairus' daughter

Jairus, a synagogue leader, asked Jesus to come to heal his daughter who was dangerously ill. Jesus was interrupted on the way by a woman with a haemorrhage (internal bleeding) (see below). As they approached Jairus' house some servants brought the message, 'Your daughter is dead, why bother the teacher any more?' Jesus told Jairus not to be afraid, but to believe. When they arrived, Jesus commented on the loud weeping outside the house. He told them that the child was not dead, only sleeping. He took Peter, James and John inside along with the girl's parents. Jesus took the girl by the hand and said, 'Talitha koum!' (Aramaic for 'Little girl, I say to you, get up!') The girl immediately got up. Jesus told them to give her something to eat. He said that they must tell nobody about the miracle.

The key to the miracle was faith – note that Jesus said to Jairus, 'Don't be afraid, just believe.' The faith that saved the girl was the faith of her parents. In the next miracle it was the faith of the woman herself.

### Mark 5: 25–34. The woman with a haemorrhage/internal bleeding

As Jesus made his way to Jairus' house, a large crowd followed him. In the crowd was a woman who had been bleeding internally for twelve years. She had spent a lot of money on doctors but no one could help her. She believed that all she had to do was to touch Jesus' cloak. When she did, her bleeding stopped immediately. Jesus felt power go out of him and asked who had touched him. The woman was afraid that Jesus would be angry. Jesus said, 'Daughter, your faith has healed you. Go in peace and be freed from your suffering.'

Note that when Jesus calmed the sea he criticized the disciples for their lack of faith (Mark 4: 35–41 – see page 17).

### 1C  *Mark 9: 14–29. **The epileptic boy***

After the transfiguration, Jesus, with Peter, James and John, found the other disciples surrounded by a crowd. A man had brought his epileptic son to be healed. The disciples tried to heal the boy but they could not. The boy's father said, 'If you can do anything, take pity on us and help us.' Jesus replied, 'Everything is possible for him who believes.' The father said, 'I do believe; help me overcome my unbelief.' Jesus healed the boy. When the disciples later asked why they had been unable to heal the boy Jesus said, 'This kind can come out only by prayer.'

Another miracle in which a parent's faith saved a child is the healing of the Syro-Phoenician woman's daughter (Mark 7: 24–30 – see page 17).

Note Jesus' conversations with the boy's father and with the disciples, especially what is said about faith and prayer.

### 1D  *Matthew 14: 22–33. **Jesus walks on water***

The disciples were caught in a storm as they were crossing the Sea of Galilee by night. When they saw Jesus walking on the water towards them they were terrified, thinking he was a ghost. Jesus told them, 'It is I. Don't be afraid.' Peter tried to walk towards him but panicked and began to sink. Jesus caught him, saying, 'You of little faith, why did you doubt?'

Note what Jesus said about Peter's lack of faith.

### 1D  *Luke 7: 1–10. **The centurion's servant***

The centurion was a Roman officer. He respected the Jews (he had built them a synagogue) and they respected him. They came to ask Jesus to go to heal the servant. As Jesus approached the house, he received a message from the centurion: 'Lord, don't trouble yourself, for I do not deserve to have you come under my roof. That is why I did not even consider myself worthy to come to you. But say the word, and my servant will be healed.' He said that just as he gave orders to soldiers and servants, knowing that they would be obeyed, so Jesus could order an illness to go. Jesus was amazed by the man's faith; he completely trusted Jesus to heal his servant. Even among the Jews, Jesus had not found faith like the faith of this Roman. When the messengers returned home they found the servant had been healed.

Note what Jesus said about the centurion's faith. He was a Gentile, yet he showed greater faith than many Jews.

## 1D *Luke 17: 11–19. The men with leprosy*

**hints and tips**

Faith is the key to all these miracles. Be sure that whenever you answer a question about one of these miracles, you write about the importance of faith.

Leprosy was so infectious that lepers were not allowed near other people. So these ten lepers shouted to Jesus and asked him to heal them. Jesus told them to go and show themselves to a priest (they could not approach other people again until the priest pronounced them clean). They set off to go to the priest – which was a great act of faith in itself, since they were not yet cured. As they went they found their leprosy had left them. One of them came back to thank Jesus. Jesus commented that the one who had come back was a Samaritan, not a Jew! He told the man, 'Your faith has made you well.'

Again, Jesus pointed out that the Samaritan, a Gentile, showed more faith than the Jewish lepers.

## The importance of faith for Christians today

1   Christians facing illness.

- Christians believe that medical skill is a gift from God. In illness they pray to God for healing. They also trust doctors, nurses and hospital staff.

- Prayer for those who are ill is an important part of the Church's ministry. In many traditions there are **rites** of healing. Individuals receive the laying on of hands and the **congregation** join in praying for them.

- Some sick people make **pilgrimages** to **holy** places to pray for healing. See the section on pilgrimage on pages 85–86.

- Christians do not regard prayer as a quick fix, by which a cure for illness is guaranteed. They pray for strength to cope with illness.

- Some Christians dedicate themselves to caring for the incurably sick. In particular, many work in the hospice movement.

2   Many Christians have problems and crises to face in everyday life. Examples include problems and tensions in the family, temptations such as drug or alcohol abuse or even the pressures of an exam.

- Christians have faith in the promise of Jesus that he will always be with them. They believe that he understands the problems they face.

- Some Christians find that, in a crisis, prayer can give them great support and strength. They may slip into a church to pray for a few minutes or simply offer a quick silent prayer wherever they happen to be.

In all these situations, Christians remember the miracles of Jesus and what he said about the importance of faith and prayer.

**read more**

See Section 10 on sacraments, pages 59–61. Anointing the sick is one of the **sacraments** among Roman Catholics and Anglicans.

## Try these short questions

1C

**a** When the disciples asked why they had been unable to heal the epileptic boy, what did Jesus reply? (2 marks)

1D

**b** How did the centurion, whose servant was healed, show his faith in Jesus? (3 marks)

1C 1D

**c** Why did the woman with a haemorrhage touch Jesus' cloak? (3 marks)

**d** After Jesus raised Jairus' daughter, what did he tell Jairus and his wife they must do and they must not do? (2 marks)

## Exam-type questions

Explain what the miracle of the raising of Jairus' daughter teaches about Jesus. (4 marks) (SEG, 1998)

### Student's answer

*Jairus' daughter was very ill. He came to find Jesus to ask him to heal her. He was very upset when Jesus stopped to cure a woman who was ill, even though she was not as ill as his daughter. A servant came to tell them that the girl had died. Jairus did not lose faith. When Jesus came to the house he sent everyone away except three disciples, Jairus and Jairus' wife. He told the girl to get up and she did. Jesus said they should give her something to eat. This shows that Jesus is the Son of God.*

### Examiner's comments

This is a very poor answer. The question did not ask the student to write out what happened, yet that is about all that has been written. Also, there is more about Jairus than Jesus. Some of the things which are said about Jairus are not in Mark's Gospel. For instance, nowhere in the Gospel does it say that he was upset when Jesus stopped to cure a woman or that he did not lose faith. The only place where the student has tried to explain what the miracle says about Jesus is in the last sentence. A mark would be given here, even though Mark does not say that everyone who heard of it believed he was the Son of God. Christians reading about the miracle might take it as proof that Jesus is God, so it would be unfair not to allow the student a mark.

The answer should have said that Mark shows Jesus responding immediately to people in need, facing a crisis. When the news of the girl's death arrived Jesus turned to support Jairus, telling him to have faith. All the time Jesus knew the girl would be healed – note how he told the mourners, 'the child is not dead, but asleep.' Jesus took witnesses into the girl's room so that they might see the miracle.

When the girl had been raised, Jesus told her parents to tell nobody about what they had seen. He did not want to be known simply as a miracle worker. His words are an example of messianic secrecy (see page 18).

Christians would see the miracle as a sign of Jesus' power over death. Mark: 1/4

### Examination practice

**a** Give a detailed account of the calming of the storm, as told by Mark. (5 marks)

**b** Explain how this story may have helped the first Christians to understand Jesus as Saviour. (3 marks)                                                                     (NEAB, 2001)

## Checklist for revision

|  | Understand and know | Need more revision | Do not understand |
|---|---|---|---|
| I can describe two miracles of healing in which faith played an important part. | ☐ | ☐ | ☐ |
| I understand the link between faith and miracles. | ☐ | ☐ | ☐ |
| I understand why faith is important to Christians today. | ☐ | ☐ | ☐ |

# 7 Discipleship

## Topic summary

- Jesus chose a special group of twelve followers, his **disciples** (sometimes called 'The Twelve').
- Jesus said that anyone who followed him, not just the Twelve, would have to be prepared to suffer.
- After the **resurrection** Jesus gave his followers a **commission** to spread the Gospel.
- Christians believe that they are called by Jesus to follow him in the same committed way.

## What do I need to know?

- A disciple is a learner. The Twelve Disciples were chosen by Jesus to be with him, to learn from him and to spread the Gospel when he returned to the Father.
- Discipleship means commitment. Christians believe that they are committed to loving and serving God and neighbour.
- The following Bible passages, including those about people Jesus met.

  **1C** Mark 1: 16–20; Mark 3: 13–19; Mark 6: 7–13; Mark 8: 34–8; Mark 10: 28–31; Mark 12: 41–4; Mark 14: 26–31, 66–72; Mark 16: 14–18

  **1D** Matthew 12: 9–14; Matthew 13: 1–46; Matthew 14: 22–33; Matthew 25: 14–46; Mark 1: 14–20; Mark 2: 23–8; Luke 5: 17–26; Luke 5: 27–32; Luke 7: 36–50; Luke 19: 1–10

  **2B** Matthew 13; Matthew 20: 24–8; Matthew 28: 18–20; Mark 12: 41–4; Luke 5: 1–11, 27–32; Luke 10: 25–37

## The Twelve Disciples

Note that when Jesus called the disciples he told them they must leave everything and come right away: they obeyed.

**read more**

**2B** Luke 5: 1–11 describes the call of Peter in more detail.

### 1C 1D *Mark 1: 16–20. The calling of the first disciples*

When Jesus called the first two disciples (Simon Peter and Andrew), he said he would make them fishers of men. They left everything to follow him, as did two other fishermen, James and John, sons of Zebedee.

### 1D *Luke 5: 27–32. The calling of Levi*

Levi was a tax collector. Tax collectors were social outcasts because

- they collected taxes for the Romans – foreign invaders
- they were suspected, very often with good reason, of being dishonest and taking extra money which they kept for themselves.

When Jesus called Levi, he left his work and followed Jesus. Some people were surprised that Jesus chose a tax collector as a disciple. They criticized Jesus for having a meal with Levi and his friends. Jesus answered, 'It is not the healthy who need a doctor, but the sick. I have not come to call the righteous, but sinners to repentance.' Other people would have nothing to do with tax collectors and other outcasts. Jesus accepted them and offered them friendship.

### 1C  *Mark 3: 13–19.* **The appointing of the twelve apostles**

Note the reasons Mark gives to explain why Jesus chose twelve disciples.

- That they might be with him.
- That he might send them out to preach.
- To have authority to drive out demons.

**hints and tips**

Think about why the disciples left everything to follow Jesus.

### 1C  *Mark 6: 7–13.* **Crowds follow Jesus**

Jesus sent the Twelve out in pairs on a mission. He said they should only take a staff with them – no food or money. Where they found a welcome they were to stay; if they were not welcome, they should shake the dust off their feet. They went out and preached that people should repent. They healed many sick people.

## Discipleship is demanding

### 1C  *Mark 10: 35–45*  2B  *Matthew 20: 24–8.* **The request of James and John**

The mother of James and John asked Jesus to promise that her sons should have the chief places in the kingdom of heaven. (In Mark, the two disciples themselves ask him.) The other ten disciples were indignant. Jesus told them that standards in the kingdom were not the same as in the everyday world. They should not aim for high status and important positions. They had to be ready to serve and suffer – just as he, the Son of Man, came to serve others and to give his life to ransom people from their sins.

### 1C  *Mark 8: 34–8*

Anyone who wants to follow Jesus must be prepared to take up the cross – in other words, to suffer.

### 1C  *Mark 10: 28–31*

Those who are prepared to put Jesus above everything – even family, home and possessions – will find that they still have family and home in this life, though there will be persecution. They are also promised everlasting life.

### 1C  *Mark 14: 26–31, 66–72.* **Peter's promise and denial**

After the Last Supper, Jesus warned the disciples that they would all desert him. Peter insisted that he would never desert him. Jesus told him that before the cock had crowed twice Peter would three times deny that he knew Jesus. After Jesus was arrested Peter was in the High Priest's courtyard. Three times people said he was one of Jesus' followers, and each time he denied it. The cock crowed for the second time. Peter realized what he had done. He broke down in tears.

## The Great Commission

### 1C  *Mark 16: 14–18*

Jesus told the disciples to go through the whole world **preaching** the Gospel. They would be given power to perform **miracles**. Those who believed and were baptized would be saved. Those who would not listen would be condemned.

### 2B  *Matthew 28: 18–20*

He told them to make disciples of all nations. They were to baptize in the name of the Father, the Son and the Holy Spirit. He gave them the promise, 'I am with you always, to the very end of the age.'

## People Jesus met

The first two examples of people who wanted to follow Jesus were social outcasts – rejected by society as a whole. Jesus accepted them.

### 1D  *Luke 7: 36–50. The sinful woman*

A Pharisee called Simon invited Jesus for a meal. A sinful woman came in and, weeping, washed Jesus' feet with her tears and poured perfume over them. Simon commented that if Jesus were a prophet he would realize that the woman was a sinner and have nothing to do with her. Jesus told him a parable.
Two men owed money to the same lender. One owed ten times more than the other. Neither could pay so he forgave them both. Which would love him more? Simon replied, 'I suppose the one who had the bigger debt cancelled.'
Jesus compared the way the woman showed her love with the offhand manner in which Simon had received him. Simon had not offered Jesus water for his feet or oil to anoint himself and had not kissed him – all part of the polite way of welcoming a guest. The woman had kissed his feet, washed them with her tears and anointed them with perfume. Jesus said her sins were forgiven. This upset people – only God could forgive sins.

### 1D  *Luke 19: 1–10. Zacchaeus the tax collector*

Zacchaeus wanted to see Jesus. Because he was very small he could not see over the crowd so climbed a tree to see Jesus. Jesus told him to come down, since he wished to visit him. There were mutterings from those who did not approve of Jesus visiting a tax collector. Meanwhile, Zacchaeus told Jesus that he would give half his goods to the poor and to anyone he had cheated he would give back four times what he had taken. Zacchaeus had repented – had a change of heart – and Jesus accepted him.

On tax collectors, see the note on Levi, page 47.

read more

**1C** **2B** *Mark 12: 41–4. The widow at the treasury*

Jesus saw many wealthy people putting large sums into the treasury. A poor widow put in a very small sum. Jesus said she had put in more than anyone. The others had plenty to give and would not miss the money. She had put in all she had – she had made a real sacrifice.

## Discipleship today

Christians are committed to following the teaching of Jesus.

- In the commission, which he gave his followers after the resurrection (see above), Jesus told them to spread the good news. Many Christians today try to do as Jesus said.

- Some Christians dedicate themselves to making the Gospel known. They believe they have a **vocation** to serve God in a particular way. They may believe they are called to a particular task in the ministry of the Church as, for instance, a priest or nun. Their work will include teaching people about the Christian **faith**, leading them in worship and guiding them in the way they live as Christians.

- Others will feel a vocation to be Christians in an ordinary occupation. A nurse, teacher, telephonist, shop assistant, computer technician or a person looking after home and family – anyone can have a vocation. Whatever the way of life, a person can live and work by Christian standards.

- Note this **prayer**, which the **congregation** say together at the end of an Anglican Eucharist:

  Send us out in the power of your spirit
  to live and work to your praise and glory.

  They go out to live as Christians in the world.

- Jesus gave his followers two great commandments – love God and love your neighbour. Remember, if you love a person you will go out of your way to please that person, to give pleasure. Loving means giving committed service.

**read more** See the section on prejudice and discrimination (pages 135–140).

### Try these short questions

**1C** **1D**

a What did Jesus say to Simon and Andrew when he called them to be his disciples? What did he mean? (3 marks)          (NEAB, 1997)

**1C**

b In the commission he gave them after the resurrection Jesus told his disciples to 'preach the Gospel'. What is meant by 'preach the Gospel'? (2 marks)

(NEAB, 2000)

c Why did Jesus praise the widow who put two small coins into the temple treasury? (2 marks)          (NEAB, 1997)

## Exam-type questions

**a** Suggest three different kinds of hardships which Christians today might face when telling people about Jesus. (3 marks)

**b** What do Christians today believe are the rewards of becoming disciples of Jesus? (You may use Jesus' teaching to help your answer.) (4 marks)                    (NEAB, 2000)

### Student's answer

*a   1   Being laughed at   2   In some countries, having your church bombed*
*3   Not getting as good a job as you would have done*
*b   Jesus said the reward for being his disciple is eternal life. Christians today believe in life*
*after death and they believe in heaven. The idea of heaven must make them want to follow*
*Jesus so that they can go there. Another thing is that it makes them feel good.*

### Examiner's comments

**a** All three answers are genuine examples of hardships. The first might apply in some situations in the United Kingdom, with young Christians being ridiculed by their peers. The student may remember a bombing incident such as the one in Pakistan in 2002. The bombing was the work of extremists and such an event may not happen very often but it is a fair example. There is discrimination against Christians in work in some countries; the answer is accepted even though it may not be the case in the United Kingdom. Each answer is worth one mark.          Mark: 3/3

**b** The student has made two points, each of which could receive two marks. The first point is well made and would receive both marks. The second point is very weak and would not receive a mark. If the student had said that Christians might feel a sense of fulfilment or that they would know they were keeping the commandment 'Love your neighbour', then credit would be given.          Mark: 2/4

## Examination practice

'To be a follower of Jesus is too demanding.' Do you agree? Give reasons for your answer, showing you have thought about more than one point of view. (5 marks)          (NEAB, 1999)

# Checklist for revision

| | Understand and know | Need more revision | Do not understand |
|---|---|---|---|
| I know what is meant by disciple. | ☐ | ☐ | ☐ |
| I know why Jesus chose disciples. | ☐ | ☐ | ☐ |
| I can give two examples of hardships Christians face because of their beliefs. | ☐ | ☐ | ☐ |

> **Topic summary**
> - Many Christians believe they have a vocation.
> - In most Christian traditions people are said to have a vocation to leadership in the Church.
> - In some traditions, leaders are ordained. Those who are ordained have authority to exercise special roles within the Church.

## What do I need to know?
- The meaning of vocation.
- The special authority and duties of different ministers.

## Vocation

Some Christians believe that they have a **vocation** – they are called by God to serve him and others in a particular way. The word is often used of those in what are called caring professions such as missionaries, nurses, doctors and teachers.

## The ordained ministry

In many **traditions** people are chosen for roles of leadership. They may be lay people with special functions in the **Church**, such as teaching children, visiting the sick and leading Bible study groups.

Some Church leaders are ordained to positions of leadership. They are given authority by the Church and its members for special functions and tasks. For instance, Baptists and Methodists ordain ministers; other ministers lay their hands on their heads as a **symbol** of authority being passed on to them by the Church. The laying on of hands is accompanied by prayer for **grace** and the gift of the Holy Spirit.

Roman Catholics, Orthodox and Anglicans believe that Holy Orders is a **sacrament** (see page 59). The grace of orders has been passed on through the Church from the time of the apostles to the present day. Bishops, priests and deacons are ordained by laying on of hands into the Apostolic Succession. Through it they receive grace and the power of the Holy Spirit.

- A deacon can lead **worship**, preach, take funerals, baptize and marry people.
- A priest can also celebrate the Eucharist, give a blessing and absolve people from their sins in God's name.
- Bishops normally are the leaders of large areas called dioceses. They have authority to ordain deacons, priests and bishops. A bishop usually leads a confirmation service (pages 70–72).

> **hints and tips**
>
> Make clear that any Christian may have a vocation to serve God in any occupation or way of life. A Christian professional footballer or pop star could be a role model for young people.

Monks (who may be priests) and nuns are said to be in religious orders. The orders may be either active (with a ministry in the everyday world) or contemplative (with a life of silence and prayer in the monastery or convent).

Ministers of all traditions

- lead worship
- preach and teach
- baptize or in some other way admit and welcome new members
- have a pastoral ministry of care among the people of the Church
- visit sick and housebound people, to pray with them and, in some traditions, to take them Holy Communion
- take a leading role in the everyday running of the Church community
- prepare couples for marriage and conduct the marriage **ceremony**
- visit and support bereaved families and conduct the funerals of their loved ones.

**! beware**

Roman Catholics, Orthodox and Anglicans have priests. Other traditions speak of ministers. Be sure to use the correct title.

*Priests and nuns play an important role in the pastoral work of the Church.*

## Try these short questions

**a** Describe two functions or duties of a Christian priest or minister. (4 marks)

**b** Why do some Christian traditions (denominations) not have specially chosen (ordained) ministers? (4 marks)                    (NEAB, 2001)

## Exam-type questions

'Ministers should not wear special clothes but dress in the same way as lay people.' Do you agree? Give reasons for your answer. Show that you have thought about more than one point of view. (5 marks)                                                   (NEAB, 2001)

### Student's answer

*I think sometimes it is important for ministers to wear special clothes. It means people can recognize them easily. After all, they are ministers all the time. The special clothes show they are devoted to God and follow their faith. However, if a minister is visiting someone or just talking to them it is better that he is on their level or equal. It may put people off if they feel inferior. They may find it harder to confide in someone if they seem too distant.*

## Examiner's comments

The student has given two points of view. Wearing the clothes makes them recognizable and shows commitment. The student could have added that many people find it easier to approach a minister who is a stranger because they know what he or she stands for. To other people the clothes are a barrier; they feel embarrassed since they think ministers are not like other people. Also, the student has not made a distinction between special vestments worn for worship and distinctive clothing worn in public.                                                   Mark: 3/5

## Examination practice

Choose **two** of the following occupations. In what ways can Christians regard them as vocations? Police, veterinary surgeon, shop assistant, soldier, social worker. (8 marks)

# Checklist for revision

| | Understand and know | Need more revision | Do not understand |
|---|---|---|---|
| I know what Christians mean by vocation. | ☐ | ☐ | ☐ |
| I know the duties of ministers of different traditions. | ☐ | ☐ | ☐ |

# 9 The day of rest

## Topic summary

- The **Sabbath** (Saturday) is the Jewish **holy** day, a day of rest. It marks God's rest after the **creation** of the world.
- Christians celebrate Sunday as their holy day because Jesus rose from the dead on a Sunday. Every Sunday is a celebration of the resurrection.
- For Christians, Sunday is the day on which time should be set aside for the worship of God.

## What do I need to know?

- **1C** **1D** What Sabbath is. Why and how Jews keep Sabbath.
- Bible passages from your option, showing Jesus' attitude to Sabbath.
  - **1C** Mark 1: 21–8; Mark 2: 23–8; Mark 3: 1–6
  - **1D** Matthew 12: 9–14; Mark 2: 23–8
- Why Christians keep Sunday, not Saturday, as their holy day.
- How Christians today keep Sunday.

## The Jewish Sabbath

- 'Sabbath' is a Hebrew word meaning 'rest'.
- Sabbath is the day of rest in Judaism. It begins at sunset on Friday and lasts until sunset on Saturday.
- In the Ten Commandments the reason given for the Sabbath being a holy day is that after God had created the world in six days he rested on the seventh.
- Jews keep Sabbath as a holy day set aside for God. It is celebrated at home with a special family meal on Friday evening and with synagogue worship. Unnecessary work is avoided. Sabbath is a day to be honoured and enjoyed as a gift from God.

## Sunday – celebration of the resurrection

Christians observe Sunday as a holy day because it is the day of the resurrection. To Christians, the resurrection of Jesus is the greatest event in history.

## The teaching of Jesus

- Jesus took Sabbath seriously and worshipped in the synagogue on the Sabbath.
- Jesus and his disciples were sometimes accused of breaking the Sabbath by doing what the Pharisees regarded as work.
- Jesus taught that the Law of God was for the benefit of the human race, not a set of petty restrictions. He was not breaking the Law when he healed on the Sabbath because it was obviously the right, loving thing to do.

**read more**

Why the resurrection is so important to Christians, see pages 31–2.

**! beware**

Do not say that Christians keep Sunday as their holy day because God rested on the seventh day after creating the world. Sunday is a celebration of the resurrection.

● These incidents raised the question of authority. If Jesus was the Son of Man, sent by God, then he had authority to say how the Sabbath should be kept.

### 1C Mark 1: 21–8. The man with an evil spirit

Jesus went to the synagogue on the Sabbath and taught. It was quite normal for anyone in the synagogue to address the congregation. People were amazed at his teaching. He taught like a **rabbi,** not an ordinary teacher of the Law.
A man with an evil spirit (what people now recognize as mental illness) called out, 'What do you want with us, Jesus of Nazareth? Have you come to destroy us? I know who you are – the Holy One of God.' Jesus sent the evil spirit away. People were more amazed. Even the evil spirits obeyed Jesus.

Apparently here, at the beginning of Jesus' ministry, no one objected to Jesus healing a man on the Sabbath, even in a synagogue. Later, when religious leaders began to see Jesus as a threat to their authority, objections were made.

Other significant events took place on a Sunday (the first day of creation, the coming of the Holy Spirit at Pentecost). They are not reasons for Sunday being the Christian holy day.

### 1C 1D Mark 2: 23–8. Going through the cornfields

As Jesus and the disciples walked through the cornfields the disciples picked ears of corn. Some religious leaders criticized the disciples (not Jesus himself) because they were technically working – harvesting – on the Sabbath. Jesus replied by talking about a time when King David and his men broke the Law, by eating some of the holy bread at a shrine. The Law said only priests were allowed to eat it, but David had no food and a priest gave it to him because there was nothing else. The Law was there to protect the rights of the priests, not to stop priests feeding hungry men. 'The Sabbath was made for man, not man for the Sabbath,' said Jesus. The Law was to allow people to rest and worship God, not to stop them nibbling ears of corn.

### 1C 1D Matthew 12: 9–14, Mark 3: 1–6. The man with the withered hand

Note the small differences between the two versions. Make sure you know the Bible passage for your option. The Pharisees and others were watching Jesus to see how he reacted when he saw the man with a withered (shrivelled) hand. Knowing what they were thinking, Jesus challenged them – what does the Law say?

When the Pharisees did not reply, Jesus told the man to stretch out his hand. The hand was healed – but, far from marvelling at what was done, the enemies of Jesus began to plot his death.

## How Christians keep Sunday

● Sunday is the day for worship. Many Christians regard it as important to worship together on Sundays unless it is impossible.

● Sunday remains the main regular day for worship, celebrating the resurrection of Jesus. In many churches there are some services on weekdays; they are usually quieter and attended by fewer people.

**hints and tips**

Jesus asked the Pharisees, 'Which is lawful on the Sabbath, to do good or to do evil?'

**hints and tips**

Jesus said, If any of you has a sheep and it falls into a pit on the Sabbath, will you not take hold of it and lift it out? How much more valuable is a man than a sheep!

- Many Christians believe that Sunday should be different from other days. They accept that some work is necessary but, as far as possible, Sunday should be a day when people can relax and when families can be together.

- Some Christians believe that Sunday should be a day of rest, like the Sabbath. They assume that the commandment applies to the Christian Sunday and that on that day nobody should work unnecessarily.

- Other Christians prefer to be positive. As long as Christians give some time to worship on Sundays, what they do with the rest of the day does not matter.

## Try these short questions

**a** What is Sabbath? (2 marks)

`1C`

**b** Why were the people in the synagogue impressed when Jesus preached on the Sabbath? (2 marks)

`1C` `1D`

**c** What did Jesus ask the people in the synagogue before he healed the man with the withered hand? Why did he ask those questions? (4 marks)

## Exam-type questions

'People who are able to worship in church on a Sunday, but do not do so, cannot be called Christians.' Do you agree? Give reasons for your answer, showing that you have thought about more than one point of view. (5 marks)                                    (NEAB, 2000)

### Student's answer

*I do not agree with this statement. Someone might be ill and not able to get to church. It is not their fault, so why should they not still be called Christians? Another thing is that even if you do not go to church you can be a Christian. It is up to you what you believe. On the other hand, some people think that it is very important to worship on Sundays. It is so important that if you do not go to church you cannot call yourself a Christian.*

### Examiner's comments

This is a very poor answer, though typical of what many students write. The question is about those who are able to worship, so to write about those who are not able to do so is a waste of time. 'Even if you do not go to church you can be a Christian' is simply saying 'Yes, I agree', without giving a reason. To write, 'It is up to you what you believe' is pointless. Christians have definite beliefs and people who do not hold those beliefs are not Christians. The last two sentences simply say that some people would disagree with the statement, again without giving any reason at all.    Mark: 0/5

## Examination practice

**a** Explain why the Pharisees criticized Jesus and his disciples as they walked through a cornfield. (2 marks)

**b** Give two reasons why Christians today believe that it is important to keep Sunday as a day of rest. (2 marks)                                                                    (NEAB, 1997)

## Checklist for revision

|  | Understand and know | Need more revision | Do not understand |
|---|---|---|---|
| I know how and why Jews keep the Sabbath. | ☐ | ☐ | ☐ |
| I can describe two events in the life of Jesus which happened on the Sabbath. | ☐ | ☐ | ☐ |
| I know why Christians keep Sunday as their holy day. | ☐ | ☐ | ☐ |

# 10 The Sacraments

## Topic summary

- A sacrament is a means by which Christians may access the grace of God.
- In each sacrament something is said or done which is a sign of the gift of God's grace.
- This section concentrates on the sacraments of healing – **Reconciliation** and Anointing of the Sick.

## What do I need to know?

- What a sacrament is.
- What the seven sacraments are and why they are important to many Christians.

## The sacraments

Christians believe that God offers to his followers his grace, a gift of his power and love, to support and guide them in their Christian lives. While there is no limit to the ways in which God may give grace to a person, the sacraments are channels through which grace may be found. In each sacrament there is a sign, which can be seen or heard. The sign indicates that God, who cannot be seen or heard, is present and active in giving his grace.

Roman Catholics, Orthodox and many Anglicans practise seven sacraments.

> **hints and tips**
>
> When writing about sacraments, explain that each one is a channel of God's grace.

| Sacrament | Signs which are seen and/or heard |
|---|---|
| Baptism | Water; the words 'I baptize you in the name of the Father and of the Son and of the Holy Ghost.' |
| Confirmation | The bishop lays hands on or stretches hands over the candidate; chrism (optional for Anglicans). |
| Eucharist | The bread and wine; the words of Jesus, 'This is my body ... this is my blood.' |
| Reconciliation | Contrition, confession and satisfaction from the penitent; **absolution** from the priest. |
| Anointing of the Sick | The laying on of hands; the use of oil and the words of anointing. |
| Marriage | The vows of the husband and wife. |
| Orders | The bishop lays hands on or stretches hands over the candidate and speaks the words of ordination. |

> **did you know?**
>
> Baptism and Eucharist are called **Dominical Sacraments** because Jesus told his followers to baptise and to celebrate communion.

- Sacraments of **Initiation** (*Baptism, Confirmation, and Eucharist*). Christians receive the risen Christ to give them power to live their everyday lives.
- Sacraments of Healing (*Reconciliation and Anointing of the Sick*). These sacraments offer the grace of forgiveness through God's love and grace to face illness of body and mind. In this section the Roman Catholic **rites** are described.
- Sacraments of Vocation and Service (*Marriage and **Holy** Orders*). Christians receive grace to contribute in special ways to Church and society.

**read more** Pages 67–70 (baptism), 70–2 (confirmation) and 62–6 (Eucharist)

# Sacraments of Healing
## *Reconciliation*

Three things are essential from the penitent:

- contrition, genuine sorrow and repentance
- personal confession of sin before a priest
- satisfaction, which in this context means 'putting things right'.

**read more** See pages 127–30 (marriage) and 52–4 (Holy Orders)

The sacrament is seen as important because not only do penitents confess and receive forgiveness for their sins, their relationship with God is restored. The usual way of receiving this sacrament is through **absolution** given by a priest.

- Penitents spend time preparing by thinking of the sins they have committed since their last confession.
- They go to the priest. The penitent may be in a small room with a small grille separating it from where the priest is sitting. They may simply sit in the same room.
- The priest prays for the penitent and may read from the Bible.
- The penitent confesses to the priest, making clear the extent of each sin and how often it has been committed.
- The priest may offer advice. He may give a **penance**, such as a prayer to be said. This is a form of satisfaction or making amends for sin. Another form of making satisfaction is to make good any harm one has done.
- The priest pronounces absolution and blesses the penitent.

*A priest with a penitent.*

## *Anointing of the Sick*

The basis of the sacrament is in

- the healing **miracles** of Jesus, signs of love and care for those who suffer. Note how, when healing the paralysed man, Jesus said, 'Your sins are forgiven', before saying, 'Take up your bed and walk.' (Mark 2: 1–12)
- James 5: 13–15. 'Is any one of you sick? He should call the elders of the church to pray over him and anoint him with oil in the name of the Lord. And the prayer offered in faith will make the sick person well; the Lord will raise him up. If he has sinned, he will be forgiven.'

The sacrament may be administered to anyone who is ill. The sick person may be facing an operation or have a long term illness or be near to death; the nature and severity of the illness will be reflected in the words of the prayers. The purpose of the sacrament is to reassure the sick person that God loves and cares.

- Prayers of penitence are said. The priest may hear the sick person's confession. There are Bible readings.
- In silence the priest lays hands on the sick person.
- The sick person is anointed on his forehead and hands, the priest saying, 'Through this holy anointing and his great love for you, may the Lord help you by the power of his Holy Spirit. May the Lord who frees you from sin save you and raise you up.'
- The sick person receives Holy Communion and is blessed by the priest.

**hints and tips**

When writing about a sacrament, mention both the outward sign and the spiritual power.

## Try these short questions

**a** What did James write about anointing the sick? (2 marks)

**b** In the Sacrament of Reconciliation, what is meant by

**i** contrition? **ii** satisfaction? (4 marks)

## Exam-type questions

Explain why Roman Catholics believe that it is important to receive the sacrament of the Anointing of the Sick. (4 marks)                    (NEAB, 2001)

### Student's answer

*They believe that the sacrament helps the person by showing them that God loves them. Part of the sacrament is when they ask forgiveness for their sins and God forgives them because he loves them. Anointing is taken from what James says in the Bible, that the priests will anoint people who are ill. It may make them feel good and even make them better.*

### Examiner's comments

The first two sentences are accurate and relevant. James says that the elders will not only anoint the sick but pray for them as well. The purpose is not just to make them feel good. The sacrament is the means by which they receive God's grace.                    Mark: 2/4

## Examination practice

'I don't see the point of confessing your sins to a priest. Surely God can just forgive your sins in private.' How far do you agree?  (4 marks)                    (SEG, 2000)

# Checklist for revision

| | Understand and know | Need more revision | Do not understand |
|---|---|---|---|
| I know what is meant by sacrament. | ☐ | ☐ | ☐ |
| I can name the seven sacraments and I know the outward sign of each of them. | ☐ | ☐ | ☐ |
| I can describe and explain the Sacraments of Healing. | ☐ | ☐ | ☐ |

# 11 Holy Communion

## Topic summary

- At the Last Supper Jesus gave his disciples bread and wine, telling them they were his body and blood. He told them, 'Do this in memory of me.'
- Christians understand Holy Communion in different ways.
- The Eucharist is celebrated in different ways by different traditions.
- The Salvation Army and the Quakers do not have Holy Communion services.

## What do I need to know?

- What happened at the Last Supper (Mark 14: 12–25).
- Why Holy Communion is important to Christians.
- Different ways in which Christians understand Holy Communion.
- How different traditions celebrate the Eucharist.

## Why does the service have so many names?

The names used to describe a Holy Communion service emphasize different ways in which Christians understand its meaning. The use of a name does not mean that Christians of that tradition do not accept beliefs which are emphasized by other names. All these names represent beliefs that are shared by Christians of many traditions.

- *Holy Communion*. A bond with Jesus himself and with their fellow Christians.
- *Eucharist*. Christians thank God for the blessings which come from the death and resurrection of Jesus (Roman Catholics and Anglicans).
- *Mass*. Strengthened by the body and blood of Jesus and by the fellowship of the Church, Christians go out with a mission to the world. The Latin Mass ended with the words '*Ite, missa est*' – 'Go, you are sent on a Mission' (Roman Catholics and some Anglicans).
- *The Lord's Supper*. As Jesus shared the Last Supper with his disciples, so he is spiritually present among his followers today (Methodists and Baptists).
- *The breaking of bread*. A fellowship meal which Christians share in memory of the death and resurrection of Jesus.
- *Liturgy*. The service Christians offer to God. Orthodox Christians use the name because at the **Divine Liturgy** they offer God their praise and worship. They also offer him their everyday lives.

## The Last Supper

Mark (14: 12–25) describes how Jesus ate the Passover meal with his disciples.

He sent two disciples into Jerusalem with orders to follow a man carrying a jar of water (an unusual sight – this was women's work). They were to ask the owner of the house to which the man went, 'The Teacher asks: "Where is my guest room, where I may eat the Passover with my disciples?"' He would show them a large upstairs room where they could get everything ready for the Passover meal.

In the evening Jesus and the rest of the disciples arrived. Jesus told them that one of them was going to betray him. 'Surely not,' they said, but Jesus was clear – one of those dipping in the dish with him would betray him. It was all part of God's plan – in the **scriptures** it had been said that the Son of Man would be betrayed. That did not make the person who did it any less a traitor. It would have been better if he had never been born.

Jesus took bread, gave thanks, broke it and gave it to them. 'Take it; this is my body,' he told them. He took the cup, gave thanks and passed it to each of them. He told them, 'This is my blood of the **covenant**, which is poured out for many.' He went on with some puzzling words, 'I tell you the truth, I will not drink again of the fruit of the vine until that day when I drink it anew in the **kingdom of God**.' Here Jesus apparently meant the kingdom of God in heaven.

## The meaning of Holy Communion

- At Holy Communion Christians remember Jesus. As they receive the bread and wine they remember his words: 'Do this in memory of me.'
- The risen Christ is present among the worshippers in a real and special way. They share a meal of fellowship with him and with each other.
- Jesus said that the bread and wine were his body and blood. Some Christians believe that once the bread and wine at a communion service have been **consecrated** they are indeed the body and blood of the risen Christ. He is present in the bread and wine in a special way and, when people receive the consecrated bread and wine, he is present with them personally. How the bread and wine become the body and blood of Christ is regarded as a mystery. Attempts to explain what happens using words such as transubstantiation and consubstantiation are rare nowadays.
- Other Christians believe that there is no change in the bread and the wine but that Jesus is present in a unique way when his followers share in the Lord's Supper. The worshippers share a bond with him and with their fellow Christians.
- Holy Communion is more than something shared by those present at the service. The worshippers feel a bond with other Christians throughout the world. They also believe they are joining with the saints and angels in heaven as they worship God. The eucharistic (thanksgiving) prayer includes words such as:

> Therefore with saints and angels and with all the choirs of heaven,
> We join in the song of eternal praise.

> **did you know?**
>
> Passover is a Jewish religious festival. They remember the time when God saved the people of Israel from Egypt and made the Old Covenant with them. At the Last Supper, Jesus said his blood was the blood of the New Covenant. Since they left Egypt in a hurry, without their bread having had time to rise, they eat unleavened bread at Passover.

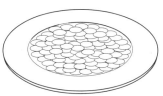

*Some Christians use unleavened bread. Jesus would have used unleavened bread at the Last Supper, a Passover meal.*

*Some Christians use ordinary bread symbolizing the idea that Jesus takes our offerings of ordinary things and changes them into something wonderful.*

- Holy Communion guides and strengthens worshippers to live as God wants them to live. They go out from the service to live and work as Christians in the world.

Note the link between Holy Communion and the everyday life of Christians. They come together to be with Jesus Christ and their fellow Christians. They go out into the world to show, in their lives, God's love for all people.

- For Orthodox, Roman Catholics and Anglicans, the Eucharist is the main act of worship every Sunday. In some churches the Eucharist is celebrated regularly on weekdays as well.
- Methodists and Baptists have a Holy Communion service once or twice monthly.
- The Salvation Army do not have Holy Communion services. Salvationists believe that it is possible to live a holy life and receive the grace of God without the use of physical sacraments. The inward experience is the most important thing.
- Quakers do not have Holy Communion services. They believe that everyone can have a direct relationship or 'communion' with God, and that this communion can best be experienced if they meet in silence, with nothing pre-planned, to wait on the Holy Spirit.

# The Roman Catholic Mass

- The priest greets the **congregation**. They ask God's forgiveness for their sins and praise God in the words of a **hymn** of praise called the Gloria.

### The Liturgy of the Word

- There are three readings from the Bible. Everyone stands for the last of them, taken from one of the **Gospels**.
- The priest preaches a homily (sermon) usually explaining one of the Bible readings.
- Everyone states their belief in God by saying the Nicene **Creed** together.
- In the Prayer of the Faithful the congregation pray for the Church, for the world, for the people of the neighbourhood, family and friends, for the sick and all who suffer, and for those who care for them and finally for those who have died, especially those who have died recently.

### The Liturgy of the Eucharist

- The bread and wine are brought to the altar.
- The priest prays over them the words of the Eucharistic prayer. He uses the words which Jesus spoke at the Last Supper.

> He gave you thanks and praise.
> He broke the bread,
> gave it to his disciples, and said:
> Take this, all of you, and eat it:
> this is my body which will be given up for you.

- He prays over the wine using similar words.
- The congregation say the Lord's Prayer.
- Priest and congregation exchange the peace by taking those around them by the hand and saying, 'Peace be with you.'

**hints and tips**

Make sure that if you are asked to describe a Holy Communion service in any tradition, you describe the whole service, including the Liturgy of the Word. If a question is marked, for example, out of eight and you only describe the consecration and communion, your mark will be four at the most.

- Members of the congregation come forward to receive communion.
- The priest blesses the congregation and says to them, 'Go in peace to love and serve the Lord.' Strengthened by the presence of the risen Christ, the congregation go out into the everyday world.

# The Divine Liturgy (Orthodox Church)

Much of the action of the Divine Liturgy takes place in the sanctuary, out of sight of the congregation. The congregation are separated from the sanctuary by the iconostasis (see page 81). The iconostasis symbolizes the divide between earth and heaven and the Royal Doors are the way by which the priest may pass through the doors, especially at the Lesser Entrance and the Greater Entrance.

## The Liturgy of the Word

- There are prayers and a reading from the Bible.
- The priest comes through the Royal Doors for the singing of the Gospel. This is known as the Lesser Entrance, when the priest brings the Gospel to the people.

## The Liturgy of the Faithful

- Bread and wine are brought. These are the gifts of the worshippers – the bread will have been baked by a member of the congregation. They are taken through the Royal Doors to the altar. This is the Greater Entrance.
- Prayers are offered for the Church, the world and the local community.
- Behind the Royal Doors, which are closed, the priest speaks the words spoken by Jesus over the bread and wine at the Last Supper.
- The bread is divided into four parts. Three parts are consecrated by the priest as the body and blood of Christ. Of those three parts, one part is placed in the wine which is in the chalice, one part is for the clergy and one part for the communion of the congregation. The remaining, unconsecrated, part is divided into small pieces.
- The priest comes through the Royal Doors and, in front of the iconostasis, distributes the consecrated bread and wine together on a spoon. Any member of the Orthodox Church who has received baptism and chrismation, even a small baby, may receive communion.
- Prayers of thanksgiving are said after the communion.
- As people leave the church the priest gives them pieces of unconsecrated bread, the antidoron.

# Holy Communion in a Methodist Church

- The service begins with a hymn and with a prayer of praise and thanksgiving.
- There are Bible readings and a sermon.
- The congregation pray for the world and for people with particular needs.
- The minister takes the bread and wine and says the Prayer of Thanksgiving over them, including the words, 'This is my body' and 'This is my blood'.
- Methodists have an 'open table'. They welcome 'all those who love the Lord Jesus Christ' to receive communion.
- The worshippers go out into the world to live to God's praise and glory.

*Most traditions distribute the consecrated wine in a chalice, a special cup or goblet usually made of silver. Some traditions prefer to use small individual glasses. Most traditions use ordinary wine, some use non-alcoholic wine.*

## Try these short questions

**a** What did Jesus say when he gave his disciples the bread and wine at the Last Supper? (3 marks)

**b** What is meant by the Liturgy of the Word at a Eucharist? (2 marks)

**c** What is the significance of the titles 'Holy Communion', 'Eucharist', 'Mass' and 'Lord's Supper'? (4 marks)

## Exam-type questions

**A** 'Give a man a fish and you feed him for a day; teach him to fish and you feed him for life.' (A phrase to explain the work of CAFOD/TRÓCAIRE)

**B** 'Go in peace to love and serve the Lord.' (The last words of the Mass)

Explain how the words of **A** are related to the words of **B**. (4 marks) (NEAB, 1999)

### Student's answer

*The quote means 'It is a good thing to feed people who are starving. It is better to teach people to feed themselves.' CAFOD does both. It sends food and other emergency supplies where they are needed and it also trains people in particular skills and supplies the equipment they need. CAFOD do this because Jesus taught us to love and serve other people. People come to Mass to show their love for Jesus. At the end the priest says to them, 'Go in peace to love and serve the Lord.' Praying for CAFOD and giving money to help the work of CAFOD is one way of loving and serving Jesus.*

## Examiner's comments

The student has explained both statements and has shown the link between the two. This is a strong answer.

Mark: 4/4

## Examination practice

Choose **one** Christian tradition/denomination in which Holy Communion is celebrated.

**a** Describe a Holy Communion service in the tradition you have chosen. (8 marks)

**b** Explain how what is said and done in the service shows the meaning and importance of Holy Communion in that tradition. (7 marks) (AQA, 2002)

## Checklist for revision

| | Understand and know | Need more revision | Do not understand |
|---|---|---|---|
| I can give an account of the Last Supper. | ☐ | ☐ | ☐ |
| I can describe a Eucharist in three different traditions. | ☐ | ☐ | ☐ |
| I understand the importance of Holy Communion for Christians of different traditions. | ☐ | ☐ | ☐ |

# 12 Initiation rites

## Topic summary

- Jesus was baptized by John the Baptist in the river Jordan.
- Jesus told his followers to baptize people in the name of the Father, the Son and the Holy Spirit.
- Baptism is a means of **initiation** into the Christian **faith**.
- Some Christians believe that baptism is a precious gift from God and that it is important to baptize children so that they may share this gift. Commitment should follow when the child is old enough to understand and choose.
- Other Christians believe that baptism should not take place until the person being baptized can understand what they are doing, choose to be baptized and make a commitment to Jesus Christ.
- Some Christians do not baptize. They see no need for symbolic actions or ceremonies.
- Baptism is carried out in one of two ways.
  1 Water is poured on the forehead.
  2 Baptism by total immersion – the person's body is totally immersed in water.
- In some traditions, at confirmation, Christians receive the gift of the Holy Spirit. Among Orthodox Christians, confirmation, known as chrismation, immediately follows baptism. In other traditions people are confirmed when they are old enough to understand and make a personal commitment.

## What do I need to know?

- Infant baptism; believers' baptism.
- **1A** Chrismation, dedication; confirmation.
- **1B** Chrismation; confirmation.

## Baptism in the New Testament

- John the Baptist baptized in the river Jordan. He taught that before being baptized people must repent. If they repented and were baptized, their sins would be forgiven. The **Messiah** was coming. The way to prepare for his coming was to repent and be baptized.
- Jesus was baptized by John – see page 15. Matthew in his Gospel says that John was reluctant to baptize Jesus. Jesus had no sin and did not need to repent.
- After the resurrection Jesus told his disciples to 'make disciples of all nations, baptizing them in the name of the Father and of the Son and of the Holy Spirit'.

- On the day of Pentecost, Peter told people in Jerusalem to repent and be baptized for the forgiveness of their sins. 3000 were baptized that day.
- Baptism was often followed by the laying on of hands. Through the laying on of hands, apparently by the apostles, the Holy Spirit was given. Read Acts 8: 14–17. Some people in Samaria became Christians and were baptized. The local Church asked two of the apostles, Peter and John, to come to lay hands on them so that they might receive the Holy Spirit.
- Paul described baptism as dying with regard to sin and rising to new life with Jesus.

## Infant baptism

Infant baptism is normal among Roman Catholics, Anglicans, Orthodox, Methodists and the United Reformed Churches.

**hints and tips**

Note that in these traditions people of any age may be baptized if they have not been baptized before.

- At baptism children are welcomed into the Church. It is important to the parents that their children are brought up as members of God's family.
- Baptism is the beginning of a new, eternal life. Those who are baptized are said to be born again, beginning a new life with Jesus which does not end, even when they die.
- Baptism cleanses from original sin. Original sin is a weakness in human nature which makes people likely to sin. The Holy Spirit enters the child who is baptized and gives strength to resist temptation.

Infants and young children cannot make a commitment to follow the teaching of Jesus. The commitment is made by their parents and godparents (sometimes called sponsors). Godparents are people chosen by the parents to share with them the Christian upbringing of the children. They are often family members or close friends. They ought to be people whom the parents trust to be suitable role models for the children and to encourage them to live by Christian standards.

These are the main features of the **rite** of infant baptism.

- The parents and godparents promise that they will bring the child up as a Christian. They promise to pray for the child.
- The child is signed with the sign of the cross by the priest or minister. The parents and godparents may also make the sign of the cross on the child's forehead.
- In the Roman Catholic Church the child is anointed with oil, a sign that the child is dedicated to God.
- In the Roman Catholic and Anglican traditions the water of baptism is blessed.
- The parents and godparents are joined by the whole congregation as they state their belief in God, Father, Son and Holy Spirit.
- Water is poured three times on the child's forehead as he/she is baptized in the name of the Father, the Son and the Holy Spirit.
- The parents may be handed a lighted candle, a gift to the child which symbolizes Jesus, the Light of the World, coming into the child's life. The candle is lit from the Paschal Candle, showing that the child now shares in the risen life of Jesus.
- The whole congregation welcome the child into the family of God.

- At various stages in the rite prayers are offered for the children being baptized, their parents, godparents, families and friends.

Among Orthodox Christians the child is totally immersed in the water and, straight after the baptism, there follows chrismation.

- The godparents promise on behalf of the child to turn from evil and follow Christ. They state their faith by reciting the Nicene Creed.
- The water is blessed.
- The child is anointed with chrism (holy oil).
- The child is immersed in the holy water three times, whilst being baptized in the name of the Father and of the Son and of the Holy Spirit.
- After being dried, the child is dressed in a special baptismal robe. A cross is put round the child's neck, a sign that he or she has taken up the cross of Christ.
- Chrismation or confirmation follows immediately. The child is anointed with chrism on the head, eyes, lips, ears, chest, hands and feet. Chrismation marks the seal of the Holy Spirit on the life of the child.
- After chrismation the child is carried three times round the font.
- A small lock of the child's hair is cut as a sign of dedication to God.

## *Dedication*

Baptist and Pentecostal Churches do not practise infant baptism. They have services of dedication, for which parents bring infants to the church. At the service the congregation join the family in thanking God for the child. The parents commit themselves to bringing the child up as a Christian and the congregation promise to support and help the parents to do so.

# Believers' baptism

Baptists and Pentecostalists are among the groups of Christians which practise believers' baptism.

- They believe that baptism should be the personal choice of the individual. People should understand the commitment to Jesus Christ which they are making and should personally choose to make that commitment.
- Baptism is an act of witness. Those who come for baptism have been born again – they have experienced Jesus coming to them in a way which changes their lives. They are not born again when they are baptized. They come for baptism because they have already received the experience of being born again.
- Believers' baptism is by total immersion. It takes place in a baptistry, a small pool which is centrally placed in the place of worship, or some other suitable place. The individual is, briefly, completely covered in the water.

Worship in the traditions that practise believers' baptism is non-liturgical, so services of believers' baptism vary from place to place. These are the main features of the rite of believers' baptism.

- In the sermon the minister talks about the significance of baptism. The congregation are reminded of their own commitment made at their baptisms.
- Those who are to be baptized may wear white clothes, symbolizing forgiveness of sin and new life with Jesus.
- The candidates are asked, individually, to state that they repent of their sins and have faith in Jesus Christ as Lord and Saviour. They may give **testimony**, which means that they tell everyone how they came to faith and why they have made the decision to be baptized.
- The candidate and the minister go down into the baptistry. This symbolizes the candidate leaving behind their old, sinful way of life.
- The minister says, '*Name*, because you have repented of your sins and asked for baptism, I gladly baptize you in the name of the Father and of the Son and of the Holy Spirit.' The candidate is lowered into the water and, briefly, is completely immersed. The immersion is a sign that the old way of life has died.
- The candidate comes up from the baptistry, symbolizing rising to new life with Jesus. The congregation may sing a hymn or chorus in welcome, perhaps one chosen by the candidate. Meanwhile, a friend or sponsor will be waiting with a towel to welcome the newly baptized Christian.
- The candidates go to change and then rejoin the service.

## Traditions that do not practise baptism

The Quakers and the Salvation Army do not practise baptism in any form.

- Quakers meet to wait on the Holy Spirit. **Symbol** and **ceremony** are not part of their worship.
- The Salvation Army believe that the heart of an individual's religion is a personal relationship with God. There is no need for ceremonies such as baptism.

## Confirmation

Confirmation means strengthening. Those being confirmed (the candidates) receive the gift of the Holy Spirit in a special way. They commit themselves to turning to Jesus as their Saviour and following him.

The commitment made at confirmation is the same as at adult baptism. It is the same as that made by the parents and godparents at the baptism of an infant. Those being confirmed are taking on the promises made by parents and godparents and are stating their beliefs publicly.

In the Church of England, confirmation is administered by a bishop. A bishop normally presides at a Roman Catholic confirmation, though he may delegate the authority to confirm to a priest – particularly at Easter and Pentecost, days which are considered most suitable for confirmations.

- Easter is suitable because in baptism (remember the link between baptism and confirmation) Christians rise to new life with Jesus.
- Pentecost celebrates the coming of the Holy Spirit to the Church. At confirmation the Holy Spirit comes personally to those being confirmed.

As explained already, in the Orthodox Church confirmation or chrismation immediately follows baptism. In other traditions it is important that the person is old enough to understand what confirmation means. Those being confirmed will be at least eleven years old. In some Roman Catholic dioceses the candidates are in their teens.

Anglicans and United Reformed Church members usually receive Holy Communion for the first time after they have been confirmed. For Roman Catholics, first communion comes before confirmation, usually around the age of seven, though the age varies from diocese to diocese.

Those preparing to be confirmed attend a pre-confirmation course. They study

- what Christians believe
- the Bible – in particular the importance of regular Bible reading
- the Eucharist and its meaning
- public worship
- personal prayer
- the way in which their faith should show itself in their everyday life.

In the Roman Catholic and Anglican Churches, confirmation usually takes place during a Eucharist. These are the main features of the rite.

- The confirmation comes after the **Liturgy** of the Word.
- Those being confirmed state their faith in God and their commitment to following Jesus.
- In an Anglican service, the candidates may go to the font and sign themselves with the sign of the cross with water from the font as a sign that they are renewing the commitment made at their baptisms.
- The bishop stretches his hands over those being confirmed and prays that they may receive the gifts of the Holy Spirit.

> Send your Holy Spirit upon them to be their helper and guide.
> Give them the spirit of wisdom and understanding,
> the spirit of right judgement and courage,
> the spirit of knowledge and reverence.
> Fill them with the spirit of wonder and awe in your presence.
> (Roman Catholic rite)

- One by one the candidates come to the bishop.

- In the Roman Catholic rite each candidate is accompanied by a sponsor or parent. The sponsors are Roman Catholics who are regular worshippers and who promise to support the candidates in their lives of faith. The sponsor places his or her right hand on the candidate's shoulder as a sign of support. Using chrism (holy oil) the bishop makes the sign of the cross on the candidate's forehead, saying, 'Name, be sealed with the Gift of the Holy Spirit.' The bishop may tap the newly confirmed person on the cheek as a sign of welcome.

- In the Anglican rite each candidate may be accompanied by a sponsor, a Church member who is a relative or close friend. The sponsor places his or her right hand on the candidate's shoulder as a sign of support. The bishop says, 'Name, God has called you by name and made you his own.' He then lays his hand on the head of each, saying 'Confirm, O Lord, your servant with your Holy Spirit.' Sometimes the candidates are anointed with chrism as in the Roman Catholic rite.

- The Eucharist continues. In the Anglican rite candidates are, in most cases, receiving Holy Communion for the first time.

## Try these short questions

**a** What did Jesus tell his followers about the way in which they should baptize people? (2 marks)

**b** What is chrismation? (2 marks)

**c** What is testimony? (2 marks)

**d** At what age are candidates considered old enough to be confirmed? Why is this age considered suitable? (3 marks)

## Exam-type questions

'In baptism, these children begin their journey in faith. You speak for them today. Will you care for them, and help them to take their place within the life and worship of Christ's Church?'

**a** Explain why some Christians believe that the 'journey in faith' should begin with baptism as a child. (2 marks)

**b** Explain how believers' baptism is similar to the baptism of Jesus. (2 marks)

**c** Explain **two** ways in which Jesus' baptism was a turning-point in his life. (4 marks)

**d** 'You can only be a Christian if you have been baptized.' Do you agree? Give reasons for your answer, showing that you have thought about more than one point of view. (5 marks)

(NEAB, 2001)

## Student's answer

a  Some Christians believe in baptizing children because they are in God's family from the beginning of their lives. If the parents keep the promises they will grow up as members of the Church.

b  Two ways in which believers' baptism is similar to the baptism of Jesus are that Jesus was an adult and that John dunked him in the Jordan.

c  Jesus' baptism was a turning point in his life because it was the beginning of his ministry. It was the time when a voice from heaven said, 'This is my beloved son.' So people were told for the first time that he was the Son of God.

d  I think that is a ridiculous thing to say. The Salvation Army officers have never been baptized and who can say they are not Christian? I think that what makes a Christian is what you believe and how you live. Ceremonies are not important at all.

## Examiner's comments

a  Two clear points are made.                                                    Mark: 2/2

b  One mark would be gained for saying that Jesus was an adult. The second point is very badly expressed. The student should have written that Jesus was baptized by total immersion or lowered under the water. Although the examiner would understand the word 'dunked', the mark would probably not be given. The student might also be penalized by being given a lower mark for the quality of written communication.                    Mark: 1/2

c  Two clear points are made.                                                    Mark: 4/4

d  The student has only considered one point of view which would limit the mark to three out of five straight away. The student does say what makes a person a Christian. The statement about the Salvation Army is relevant and would have been improved if the student had said why they and the Quakers do not practise baptism.                                   Mark: 2/5

## Examination practice

a  Choose **either i** infant baptism **or ii** believers' baptism. Describe what happens and explain the meaning of the symbols used during the ceremony. (8 marks)

b  'Christians should let their children choose whether they want to be baptized or not.' Do you agree? Give reasons for your answer, showing that you have thought about more than one point of view. (5 marks)                                                       (NEAB, 2001)

# Checklist for revision

| | Understand and know | Need more revision | Do not understand |
|---|---|---|---|
| I know why infants are baptized in some traditions. | ☐ | ☐ | ☐ |
| I can describe an infant baptism. | ☐ | ☐ | ☐ |
| I know why some traditions practise believers' baptism. | ☐ | ☐ | ☐ |
| I can describe a believers' baptism service. | ☐ | ☐ | ☐ |
| I know the importance of confirmation and I can describe a confirmation service. | ☐ | ☐ | ☐ |

# 13 Sources of authority

## Topic summary

Christians believe in God. They believe that he has made himself known to the human race and still does so. Christians believe that there are different ways in which they can know God and know how he wants them to live their lives. Christians accept different sources of authority to guide them in knowing God and knowing about God.

## What do I need to know?

**1A**  Sources of authority for Christians.

- The Bible
- The Apostles' **Creed** as representing a summary of Christian beliefs.

**1B**  Sources of authority for Christians, especially for Catholics.

- The Bible
- The Apostles' Creed as representing a summary of Christian beliefs
- The role of Mary
- The teaching authority of the **Church** (the **Magisterium**)
- The role of the Pope.

## The Bible

The Bible has two parts: the Old Testament and the New Testament.

The Old Testament is from the time before Jesus Christ.

- Genesis contains accounts of events from the **creation** to the life of Joseph, who became one of the most powerful men in Egypt. Joseph and his brothers and their families settled in Egypt.
- Genesis and the next four books make up the Torah, the Jewish Law. It is more than law since it contains the account of how the people of Israel escaped from Egypt and lived in the wilderness area for many years, during which time they received from God the Ten Commandments and the rest of the Law.
- A number of books tell the history of the Jewish nation. The history is unlike normal history in that God is a central figure throughout.
- A large number of books were written by prophets, announcing God's word to the people. Sometimes the prophets would say what God was going to do at some future date, for example, that one day he would send the **Messiah**.
- Other books contain thoughts on the meaning of life and the way people should live. Among these is the book of **Psalms** (worship songs).

The New Testament is about the events of Jesus' life, especially his death and resurrection.

- The four Gospels (Matthew, Mark, Luke and John) are accounts of the life and teaching of Jesus, the climax to each being his death and resurrection. Christians regard the Gospels as particularly **holy**, since they contain the words and deeds of Jesus himself.
- The Acts of the Apostles describes how the first followers of Jesus, guided by the Holy Spirit, founded the Church and preached the Gospel message.
- There are letters written by Paul, Peter, John and others to different Churches they had founded and to individual Christians.
- Revelation is a vision of heaven.

## How Christians understand the Bible

For Christians, the Bible is the Word of God. The people who wrote it were **inspired** by God. It contains important truths about God and his relationship to the human race. Christians understand the idea of the Bible as the Word of God in different ways.

- Literalists believe that every word of the Bible is literally true.
- Fundamentalists believe that the Bible is inspired and cannot contain error.
- Conservatives believe that the Bible is inspired but that it is not a scientific text.
- Liberalists believe that the truth found in the Bible is spiritual truth, not necessarily historically or scientifically accurate.

For a more detailed explanation of these ideas see page 10 in Background to the Gospels.

## How Christians use the Bible in private and public worship

- Much worship, especially non-liturgical worship, has the reading of the Bible as a main part.
- Readings from the Bible are an important part of the Eucharist. There are usually two or three readings, the last of which is from one of the Gospels.
- The book containing the Gospel reading at a Eucharist is sometimes carried in procession to the place where it is to be read, with everyone turning to face the reader. The ceremony stresses the importance of the Gospel.
- The Eucharist is based on the Last Supper. The central part of the service follows closely the accounts of the Last Supper found in the Bible.
- **Preaching** is an important part of worship. The preacher often chooses a passage from the Bible and explains its message for everyday life.
- Psalms (Old Testament worship songs) are used in Christian worship.
- Many Christian hymns and worship songs are based on the Bible.
- Many Christians read the Bible in their private worship. Lists and booklets of readings for every day help them follow a programme of regular reading.
- The Lord's Prayer is found in the Bible (Matthew 6: 9–13; Luke 11: 2–4).

The Lord's Prayer, page 89.

*Christians meet to study the Bible together.*

## The Apostles' Creed

The Apostles' Creed was written as a summary of the basic Christian beliefs.

- There is one God. There are three persons, Father, Son and Holy Spirit, but although each person is completely God, together they are one God. The three persons are known as the Trinity, which means 'three in one'.

- Jesus Christ, God the Son, took a human nature. His birth was not like any other birth because he was not a new beginning, as is an ordinary human baby, but had always existed. Mary was a virgin when Jesus was born – the Holy Spirit had caused her to be pregnant so that she would give birth to the Son of God. See the section on the person of Jesus, page 13.

- Jesus really did suffer and die. The event took place while Pontius Pilate was governor – so this is presented as a true historical event. Also, Jesus had really died – he had actually been buried. Then, on the third day he did rise again, as the scriptures had said. His life on earth ended when he ascended. He did not simply leave the earth by dying. He returned to heaven, to reign in glory with the Father. See the sections on the death and resurrection of Jesus, pages 23–32.

- God the Holy Spirit is the third person of the Trinity. Christians believe that he is active in the Church today, inspiring and encouraging Christians and offering them support and guidance.

- The Church is described as Holy and Catholic. Holy means 'set aside for God, dedicated to God'. Catholic means 'universal – the worldwide Church founded by Jesus Christ'. Christians speak of the Church as the Body of Christ; Jesus is present and active in the world through the words and actions of members of the Church.

- There is life after death. Those who have loved and served God will be with him after death. They are the Communion of Saints.

- The punishment for human sin is death. Jesus gained forgiveness for human sin by his sacrifice on the cross. Anyone who accepts Jesus as Saviour and follows him can be saved from the punishment for sin. Jesus is the 'means of salvation' – through him people can be saved.

**did you know?**

The Apostles' Creed was not written by the apostles; it was written long after they had died. It is called the Apostles' Creed because it contains teachings passed down from the apostles.

**read more**

Find the Apostles' Creed in your textbook or notes.

- At the end of the world Jesus will return as judge. For everyone, there is a judgement after death. Christians state in the creed that they believe in the resurrection of the body – but they do not mean the physical body. They think rather in terms of a spiritual body, like the resurrected body of Jesus. They will be individuals, recognizable as themselves.

## The role of Mary 1B

Most Christians believe in the doctrine of the Virgin Birth as stated in the Apostles' Creed (see above). According to the Gospels, Mary became pregnant and gave birth to Jesus through the Holy Spirit. She did not have intercourse with Joseph.

Mary is honoured as the Mother of God by the Church. She is sometimes called Theotokos, a Greek word meaning 'God-bearer'.

- Her son, Jesus, received his human nature through Mary. Calling her Mother of God stresses that Jesus is completely God and completely human.
- Mary was honoured by God when he chose her to be the mother of Jesus. If God honoured her, Christians also should honour her.

Roman Catholics look to Mary as guide and role model.

- When told that she would be the mother of God's son, Mary replied with complete obedience. She accepted God's will without hesitation.
- Mary had faith in Jesus. At the marriage feast at Cana (John 2: 1–11), when Jesus turned water into wine, Mary had no doubts. She told the servants, 'Do whatever he tells you.'
- Mary remained faithful even through pain. When Jesus was presented to God in the temple, aged 40 days (Luke 2: 22–39), Simeon told Mary, 'A sword will pierce your own soul,' a prophecy which was fulfilled when she stood by the cross and watched Jesus die.

Two festivals celebrate the beginning and end of Mary's life.

- The Immaculate Conception. The Roman Catholic Church teaches that when Mary was conceived by her mother Anne, God caused Mary to be born free from original sin. (Immaculate means spotless, completely pure.)
- The Assumption. When she died, Mary was assumed (received into heaven). There she prays for the human race.

Roman Catholics believe in Mary as Mediatrix. That means they believe she prays for the human race. They pray to her, asking her to pray for them. The prayer 'Hail Mary' is widely used by Roman Catholics.

**beware**

Do not confuse the Immaculate Conception with the Virgin Birth. The Virgin Birth refers to Mary giving birth to Jesus through the Holy Spirit. The Immaculate Conception refers to Mary being conceived free from original sin, through intercourse between her parents in the natural way.

**beware**

Roman Catholics believe in Mary as honoured above all human beings. They do not believe in her as equal to God. When they pray to her, it is to ask her to pray for them.

## The Magisterium 1B

Roman Catholics believe that the Church has the Magisterium, the authority to teach Church members what to believe. The Magisterium belongs to the whole Church. In practice, it rests with the Pope and bishops. The Magisterium includes authority to announce moral principles by which Church members should live their lives.

## The Pope  1B

Jesus said to Peter, 'You are Peter, and on this rock I will build my church … I will give you the keys of the kingdom of heaven; whatever you bind on earth will be bound in heaven, and whatever you loose on earth will be loosed in heaven.' (Matthew 16: 18) Peter was the leader of the first Christians. He became the first Bishop of Rome. The Pope is the successor to Peter. He is the head of the Roman Catholic Church.

The Pope is the spiritual guide for Roman Catholics. He exercises the Magisterium together with the bishops, among whom he is considered the first among equals (*primus inter pares*). The highest authority remains with the Pope. The law of the Church (called Canon Law) says that the Pope has 'supreme, full, immediate and universal ordinary power in the Church and he can always freely exercise this authority'.

### Try these short questions

**1A**

**a** What is the difference between the Old Testament and the New Testament? (2 marks)

**b** What is a creed? (1 mark)

**c** What does the Apostles' Creed say about the birth of Jesus Christ? (3 marks)

**1B**

**d** Why do many Christians speak of Mary as Mother of God? (2 marks)

**e** What do Roman Catholics mean by Magisterium? (3 marks)

### Exam-type questions

**a** Christians speak of the Bible as the Word of God. Describe two different ways in which Christians understand the Bible as the Word of God. (8 marks)

**b** 'The New Testament contains all a person needs for leading a Christian life.' Do you agree? Give reasons for your answer, showing that you have thought about more than one point of view. (5 marks)                                                                 (NEAB, 2001)

### Student's answer

*a* *Fundamentalist Christians believe that the Bible is the Word of God directly from him and they believe that everything in the Bible is true and really did happen. The writers of the Bible were inspired by God – that is, he showed them what to write. They believe that God's exact teaching for life is in the Bible and that no one has interfered with that teaching. Christians especially think that the parts which are about Jesus and what he said and did are the word of God.*

*The liberal view of the Bible is that God did not write it. It was written by Christians and their personalities have come through. So the Bible is not really the Word of God.*

*b* *I disagree with the statement because Jesus lived 2000 years ago and the world is very different now because of modern technology. The Ten Commandments were written a very long time ago. For instance, some people say that the laws of the Bible are against blood transfusions, but when the laws were written no one had any idea what blood transfusions were. There are no laws about things like drugs and nuclear weapons. Some Christians say that if you love God and love your neighbour that is all that matters, but I think you still need rules to say how you should live in the world today.*

## Examiner's comments

**a** This is a fair definition of the fundamentalist view. Concepts such as 'Word of God' and 'inspired' are used and clearly understood. The fundamentalist view of truth is known. An example of a passage where a fundamentalist interpretation would be important could have been given – such as the creation of the world in six days (see Genesis 1).   Mark: 3/4

The student has a vague idea that there is a difference between fundamentalist and liberal although they have got the difference completely wrong. For one thing, most of the Bible, the Old Testament, was not written by Christians – it was written before Christianity began. More importantly, they have not grasped that liberal thinkers are not out to prove the Bible is wrong. They are looking for a different sort of truth. They are looking for a spiritual message. When thinking about Genesis 1 they would not look for a scientific account of creation. They would look for a statement that God is creator and that the human race has a unique place in the universe, a special relationship with God and a responsibility for all of nature, all the **environment**. In that sense, the Bible has a message from God and could be thought of as the Word of God. This student has missed the point altogether.   Mark: 0/4

**b** The question is about the New Testament and expects the student to concentrate on the teachings of Jesus and his followers. The reference to the Ten Commandments from the Old Testament is not relevant. However, the examples given are fair ones and would gain marks. The student does consider more than one point of view. What is written about loving God and your neighbour is relevant but should have been explained. If Christians use love of God and your neighbour as principles by which to live they will not go far wrong.   Mark: 3/5

## Examination practice

**a** Describe three ways in which Christians use the Bible in public and private worship. (7 marks)

**1B**

**b** Explain how the Roman Catholic Church helps its members to deal with the problems of modern life. (7 marks)

**c** 'People should do what they think is right, not what someone else tells them to do.' Do you agree? Give reasons for your answer, showing that you have thought about more than one point of view. (5 marks)   (NEAB, 2001)

## Checklist for revision

| | Understand and know | Need more revision | Do not understand |
|---|---|---|---|
| I understand at least two different ways in which Christians think of the Bible as the Word of God. | ☐ | ☐ | ☐ |
| I know what the Apostles' Creed says about Jesus Christ. | ☐ | ☐ | ☐ |
| **1B** I know why Mary is important to Roman Catholics. | ☐ | ☐ | ☐ |
| **1B** I understand why the Pope and the Magisterium are important to Roman Catholics. | ☐ | ☐ | ☐ |

# 14 Places of worship

## Topic summary

- A place of worship is often spoken of as God's House and treated with reverence.
- Church buildings are designed for the worship that takes place in them.
- The atmosphere and the feel of the building must help people to worship.

## What do I need to know?

- The main features of church buildings of different traditions.
- The worship which takes place in those buildings.
- How the worship affects the design of the building.
- Why many Christians think it is important to have places specially for worship. Questions may be asked on Orthodox, Roman Catholic, Anglican, Methodist, Baptist and Quaker places of worship. In **1B** the main emphasis is on Roman Catholic belief and practice.

## The main features of places of worship

You may find the following features in a church building.

### A place for celebrating the Eucharist

- The main action takes place at the altar or communion table.
- The words *altar* and *table* stress different aspects of the Eucharist. The word *altar* emphasizes the sacrifice of Jesus. The word *table* emphasizes the idea of the Eucharist as a fellowship meal.

### A place for reading and preaching

- A lectern is a reading desk. A pulpit is a raised platform. Some church buildings have a lectern, some have a pulpit.
- Some church buildings have both a lectern and a pulpit. The lectern is used primarily for reading and the pulpit for preaching.
- Sometimes the person leading worship does so from the lectern or pulpit.

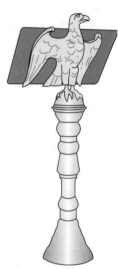

*A lectern*

### A place for baptism

- In traditions where infant baptism is the norm (for example, Orthodox, Roman Catholic, Anglican, Methodist), there is a font.
- In traditions where believers' baptism is the norm (for example, Baptist), there is often a baptismal pool (sometimes called a baptistry).
- In some traditions where baptism is not practised (for example, Quaker, Salvation Army), there is no place for baptism.

*A font*

# The focal point of a place of worship

In most places of worship there is a focal point – a central feature to which the worshipper's eye is naturally drawn. In some places there is more than one such point.

Look at the Methodist church in the picture. Notice how there are a number of features that catch the eye. The position of the pulpit shows the importance of reading the Bible and preaching. The position of the communion table shows the importance of Holy Communion. There may be a cross to remind worshippers of the importance of the death and resurrection of Jesus. The font would be in a prominent position, showing the importance of baptism in the Methodist Church.

*Inside a Methodist Church*

# An Orthodox church

- An Orthodox church is divided into two parts.
- The two parts are divided by a screen, the iconostasis. The congregation is on one side of the iconostasis and the sanctuary, where the priest leads the worship, is on the other.
- The iconostasis symbolizes the division between earth and heaven. The Royal Doors are in the centre of the iconostasis. When the priest comes through the Royal Doors it is as though the doors of heaven are opened.
- The iconostasis has many icons on it. During the Liturgy the congregation focus on the icons in their prayers.

read more

See page 65 on the Liturgy

See page 90 on icons.

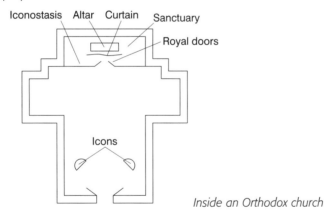

*Inside an Orthodox church*

# A Roman Catholic church

read more

See page 64 on the Mass.

- The focal point of a Roman Catholic church is the altar, where the main action of the Mass takes place.
- There is usually a large crucifix above the altar.
- Near the altar is the chair from which the service is led. The chair is seen as a symbol of the authority of Christ. The celebrant may speak or preach from the chair rather than from the lectern.
- The lectern is near the altar. It is used for the Liturgy of the Word, an essential part of the Mass.
- The tabernacle is a place (rather like a small safe) in which bread and wine, which have been consecrated at Mass, are reserved so that the sacrament can be taken

to elderly and sick people who are unable to come to the church. The tabernacle is situated near the main altar, often built into the wall. There is a light nearby, a sign that the sacrament is present. Catholics genuflect (bow) towards the tabernacle as a sign of reverence to the presence of Jesus in the sacrament.

See the section on baptism, pages 67–70.

**read more**

- Baptism, usually of infants, takes place at the font. Nowadays, it is usual for the font to be positioned where the congregation can see it, or to be moveable so that it can be brought to a central place for a baptism. It is important that the congregation together welcome the newly baptized Church member.

- Stations of the Cross – a series of fourteen stations (stopping-points) with pictures or other symbols marking stages in Jesus' passion, from his trial to his burial. Sometimes a fifteenth station is added, representing the resurrection. Worshippers move from station to station, either singly or in groups, praying and meditating at each station in turn.

- There will be statues, particularly of Mary or the Sacred Heart of Jesus. By the statues are stands for votive candles (candles lit to symbolize prayers).

- A holy water font is by the door. People sign themselves with holy water as they enter the church.

- Confessionals are small rooms, used for the Sacrament of **Reconciliation**. Traditionally, there are two rooms, with a curtain or grille between them, though often nowadays the priest and penitent sit together in the same room.

## Other places of worship

- Most Anglican churches are similar in their basic plan to Roman Catholic churches, in that the altar is the focal point of the building. There is usually both a lectern and a pulpit. Features such as statues, Stations of the Cross and confessionals are found in some Anglican churches.

- In a United Reformed Church or Methodist church the pulpit and communion table are important features. In each tradition there is a font for baptism.

- A Baptist church is similar to a Methodist church, with a baptism pool for believers' baptism.

- In a Quaker Meeting House chairs are arranged round a central table on which there is a Bible. The meeting is informal; those present sit in silence unless someone is moved by the Spirit to speak.

**hints and tips**

Always make sure that in writing about church buildings, you keep in mind what the building is for. What sort of worship takes place in it?

## Try these short questions

**a** Why is the pulpit an important feature in many church buildings? (3 marks)

**b** What is the importance of the iconostasis in an Orthodox church? (4 marks)

**c** Why is the altar the central feature in a Roman Catholic church? (2 marks)

(Based on AQA, 2002)

## Exam-type questions

Christians often make the places where they worship as beautiful as they can. Is it important that places of worship are beautiful? Give reasons for your answer, showing that you have thought about more than one point of view. (5 marks)                                   (NEAB, 1999)

## Student's answer

*It does not matter where you pray. I know of a village where the church roof needed repair so the church was closed and the people had their services in the local pub. Nobody minded and I do not suppose God did. It would be better if money was spent on houses for homeless people than on a house of God. The Bible says that God is always with Christians, wherever they are.*

*However, many Christians believe that God's house should be beautiful, in his honour. They remember how the woman anointed Jesus with expensive perfume and, when people said the money could have been given to the poor, Jesus stuck up for her. Also, it is easier to pray in a beautiful place. You feel nearer to God. You may not really be nearer to God but you might feel and think you are.*

## Examiner's comments

This student has considered more than one point of view and has given sensible arguments on each side. The example of people having services in a pub is a good one. The statement that the Bible says that God is always with Christians is vague, but there are plenty of references which could be quoted (for example, Psalm 139) and it does not matter that they are not in the syllabus. In the same way, the clear reference to the anointing of Jesus would receive credit. The arguments in favour of church buildings being beautiful are strong. The answer is not the best possible, but at GCSE level it would gain a high mark.                                   Mark: 4/5

## Examination practice

This is a drawing of the inside of a Roman Catholic church.

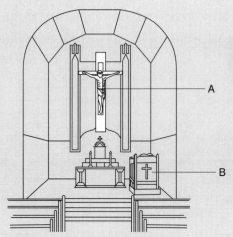

**a** Name the two features marked **A** and **B** and explain how each is used in Roman Catholic worship. (4 marks)

**b** Explain why the altar is in a central position in Roman Catholic churches. (2 marks)(NEAB, 1999)

## Checklist for revision

| | Understand and know | Need more revision | Do not understand |
|---|---|---|---|
| I know what the following features are: altar, lectern, pulpit, font, baptistry. | ☐ | ☐ | ☐ |
| I understand the importance of the iconostasis in an Orthodox church. | ☐ | ☐ | ☐ |
| I know the main features in the church buildings of these traditions and the reasons they are important: Baptist, Methodist, Anglican, Orthodox, Roman Catholic, Quaker. | ☐ | ☐ | ☐ |

# 15 Pilgrimage

## Topic summary

A pilgrimage is a journey to a holy place, for example, Lourdes or the Holy Land. Christians make pilgrimages for the spiritual experience and to offer prayers at the place of pilgrimage.

## What do I need to know?

- The reasons for **pilgrimage**.
- The study of at least one place of Christian pilgrimage.

## Why do people make pilgrimages?

- Christians visit places linked with their beliefs, for example, Bethlehem (associated with Jesus) or Lourdes (Mary). By doing so they hope to picture more clearly the events and people associated with those places. They may be filled with awe when they realize that they are really present at places which are so **holy** to them.
- Travelling is an important part of pilgrimage, even nowadays, when travel is so much easier than in the past.
- Christians travel with and meet people who share their beliefs. At the major pilgrimage sites they meet Christians from many different countries. Their faith is strengthened by becoming more aware that they are part of a worldwide fellowship.
- They step aside from the everyday world to focus more strongly on their faith.
- They may go to pray for people or needs which are important to them.

The effect of making a pilgrimage varies from person to person. Some may feel deep satisfaction that they have been able to visit and worship in holy places. They may find that when they hear passages from the Bible they can picture the sites where the events took place. Some are so moved by the experience that their faith is alive as never before. Others may find their attitude to their faith does not change at all – they continue spiritually as though the pilgrimage had never happened.

## Places of pilgrimage

### Lourdes

In 1858 a young girl, Bernadette Soubirous, had a series of visions of the Virgin Mary who told her to dig at a nearby spot. When Bernadette did so, she discovered a spring. Many Catholics believe that **miracles** of healing have occurred through the water from the spring. The authorities at Lourdes only accept claims that miracles have occurred after very careful investigation of the evidence.

*The grotto at Lourdes*

- Pilgrims visit the grotto where Bernadette saw the visions of the Virgin Mary. At the grotto pilgrims light candles and pray; the rosary is a form of prayer used by pilgrims at Lourdes.

- They visit a pool of water from the spring. They may drink the water or wash in it. Many pilgrims take bottles to fill with the water to take to friends and relatives who are ill.

- Pilgrims may attend Mass or join one of the processions. They may pray at the Stations of the Cross which are there.

## The Holy Land

Christians of all nations and traditions visit the Holy Land when it is safe to do so. It is the place where Jesus lived and taught. A pilgrimage makes the accounts of what happened more relevant, part of their own experience.

- In Bethlehem there is nothing left of the original inn or the stable. The spot on which it is believed that Jesus was born is inside the Church of the Nativity. Pilgrims go down into the small grotto where, on the floor, a silver star marks the place of Jesus' birth.

- In Jerusalem pilgrims walk along the Via Dolorosa – the route Jesus took from Pilate's judgement hall to Calvary where he was crucified. They stop to pray at the Stations of the Cross – in the original places where Jesus stopped on his way to Calvary. The Via Dolorosa leads to the Church of the Holy Sepulchre. Inside this church is the place where Jesus was crucified and, in another part of the building, the traditional place of his burial and the place where he rose from the dead.

- Elsewhere in the Holy Land Christians may visit the river Jordan and collect some water from the river in which Jesus himself was baptized. They may visit Nazareth, where Jesus lived as a child and where a huge modern church covers the traditional site of the place where the Holy Family lived. They may celebrate the Eucharist at one of the altars beside the Sea of Galilee.

## Try these short questions

**a**   What is a pilgrimage? (2 marks)

**b**   What makes Christians decide to make a pilgrimage? (4 marks)

## Exam-type questions

'Going on pilgrimage always strengthens a Christian's faith.' Do you agree? Give reasons for your answer, showing that you have thought about more than one point of view. (5 marks)   (AQA, 2001)

### Student's answer

*I think that making a pilgrimage would strengthen your faith. It must be wonderful to see places which you have read about and when you next hear the story read in church it will be easier to imagine what really happened. However, if everything is not as wonderful as you expected you might feel let down. I know someone who went on a pilgrimage and the thing that upset her was all the cheap souvenirs in the shops.*

### Examiner's comments

The student has considered arguments for and against the statement but has not really considered the feelings many pilgrims experience, of awe at what they see or fellowship with other Christians they meet. Arguments both ways could have been presented in greater depth. The student has relevantly used an experience of a friend who felt that something was lacking spiritually in the atmosphere of the place in question.                                     Mark: 3/5

## Examination practice

Explain the reasons that a pilgrim might give for going on pilgrimage. (7 marks)

# Checklist for revision

| | Understand and know | Need more revision | Do not understand |
|---|---|---|---|
| I can give reasons why people go on pilgrimage. | ☐ | ☐ | ☐ |
| I can describe a place of pilgrimage and what happens when pilgrims go there. | ☐ | ☐ | ☐ |

# 16 Prayer and worship

## Topic summary

- What is meant by prayer and worship.
- Why Christians pray and use aids to prayer.
- Private prayer, public prayer and the Lord's prayer.

## What do I need to know?

- **1A** **1B** The whole section.
- **1C** The section parts 'What is prayer?' and 'Why do Christians pray?' Bible passages: Mark 6: 45–6. Other passages in this area of option **1C** – Mark 5: 21–4 and 35–43; Mark 5: 25–34; Mark 9: 14–29 – are dealt with in the section on Jesus' teaching on faith and prayer – the **miracles** of Jesus.
- **1D** The whole section, except the parts on liturgical and non-liturgical worship.
- Bible passage: Matthew 6: 5–15

## What is prayer?

Prayer is conversation with God. Prayer includes

- adoration – adoring God and praising him
- confession – thinking about one's sins and repenting (telling God one is sorry)
- thanksgiving – thanking God
- supplication – asking God. Praying to God for other people is called Intercession.

An important part of Christian prayer is listening to God.

- Sometimes Christians use formal, set prayers written by someone else. Prayers of this sort can be found in books and collections of prayers.
- Sometimes Christians prefer extempore prayer. This means that they pray in their own words, simply expressing their thoughts and feelings to God in their own way. Extempore prayer can be used in both public and private worship.
- In **meditation**, few words are used, as the worshipper directs their thoughts towards God. Meditation can be thought of as loving God. When two people love each other, they are content just to be in each other's company.

## Why do Christians pray?

- Jesus prayed (Mark 6: 45–6) and he taught his followers to pray. In particular, he gave them the Lord's Prayer.
- Prayer is a way of approaching God and being close to him.
- Christians see their prayers as an offering to God. They offer him their praise, their thanksgiving and their love.
- Christians believe that their prayers are received through the sacrifice of Jesus on the cross. They often end prayers with words such as 'through Jesus Christ our Lord'.

**beware**

Prayer is much more than asking for things. Remember the four parts of prayer.

**hints and tips**

One way to remember the four parts of prayer is to think of ACTS of prayer. The letters stand for Adoration, Confession, Thanksgiving and Supplication.

# The Lord's Prayer

Christians regularly use the Lord's Prayer in public and private worship.

- Jesus told the disciples to use the prayer when they asked him, 'Teach us to pray.'
- It is known to Christians of every tradition.
- It is the family prayer of the Church, a symbol of unity.
- It contains different parts of prayer – adoration, confession, supplication.

*Our Father* Christians believe that they are God's children, members of his family, and that he loves them as a father.

*Who art in heaven* For Christian belief in heaven, see pages 32–3.

*Hallowed be thy name* Hallowed means holy. The words mean, may your name be treated with reverence

*Thy kingdom come. Thy will be done, on earth as it is in heaven* See the section on the **kingdom of God**. The prayer asks that people on earth will accept God as king, as do all in heaven. Another way of thinking of the prayer is, may the end of the world come so that there is no more sin and evil, but all who love God will enter heaven.

*Give us this day our daily bread* A prayer for bread, representing the basic physical needs of every human.

*And forgive us our trespasses, as we forgive them that trespass against us* A prayer for spiritual needs, for forgiveness. The prayer states that if we are to be forgiven by God, we must be ready to forgive others.

*And lead us not into temptation, but deliver us from evil* Christians do not believe that God tries to make them do wrong. Temptation here means testing. One modern translation of the Lord's Prayer reads, 'Do not put us to the test.' 'Deliver us from evil' can either mean 'Protect us from sinning, from doing evil', or 'Protect us from harm'.

*For thine is the kingdom, the power and the glory, for ever and ever* The prayer ends in praise to God.

# Aids to prayer

Some Christians make use of things to help them in their prayers. Their aim is to focus and concentrate better.

1. **Rosary.** The rosary is a method of prayer, a meditation on the birth, life, death and resurrection of Jesus. The rosary is made up of a series of mysteries based on events in the lives of Jesus and Mary.
   - The Joyful Mysteries, meditating on five events linked with the birth of Jesus.
   - The Sorrowful Mysteries, meditating on five events linked with the passion (suffering) and death of Jesus.
   - The Glorious Mysteries, meditating on five events linked with the resurrection of Jesus and his return to heaven, along with Mary's entering heaven (assumption).

**read more**

**1D** The words which follow the Lord's Prayer in Matthew 6 are: 'For if you forgive men when they sin against you, your heavenly Father will also forgive you. But if you do not forgive men their sins, your Father will not forgive your sins.'

**read more**

See the parable of the unmerciful servant, page 123.

**did you know?**

*Amen* The basic idea of 'Amen' is 'Truth'. The word comes from the Hebrew word for truth. Depending on the type of prayer, it means either 'This is true' or 'So let it be, may it be true'.

**did you know?**

Pope John Paul II has added the Luminous Mysteries, five significant moments in the life of Jesus.

The name rosary is also given to a set of beads arranged in a special way, as shown in the picture. The groups of ten beads are called decades.

Those who are praying the rosary use different prayers (Apostles' *Creed*, Our Father, Glory be and the Hail Mary) as the beads pass one by one through their fingers. During each decade they focus on one of the mysteries as they say a Hail Mary for each of the ten beads.

2. **Icon.** The word 'icon' means image. Icons are images, usually of Jesus or of one of the saints – very often of Mary. An icon is far more than a simple picture. It contains something of the nature and holiness of the person depicted.

Icons are made to be used in liturgical worship and in private prayer. Worshippers kiss the icon and sign themselves with the cross as they enter an Orthodox church. The iconostasis (see page 81) in the church is adorned with icons and during the liturgy people focus their attention on them.

*The sets of ten beads (decades) are each used for one of the mysteries.*

3. **Statues.** Statues are found in Roman Catholic and some Anglican churches. Most often seen in churches are statues of the Sacred Heart of Jesus and saints, especially Mary. Statues are certainly not worshipped. They are intended to guide people's thoughts and prayers. The Sacred Heart is a symbol of the love of God shown through the life and death of Jesus. The statues of saints remind people of the lives and example of those saints. Also, Roman Catholics and some other Christians believe that the saints, Mary among them, are constantly praying. They ask the saints to pray for them.

4. **Jesus Prayer.** 'Lord Jesus Christ, Son of God, have mercy on me, a sinner.' The Jesus Prayer is sometimes called 'the prayer of the heart'. The prayer is repeated, slowly and thoughtfully, as the thoughts and prayers of the worshipper are focused on Jesus. The use of the Jesus Prayer is a form of meditation.

5. **Candles.** The candles are lit and prayer is offered, sometimes for a special purpose or intention. Very often the candles are placed by a statue or icon. The candles symbolize the prayer which has been offered.

Do not confuse the Lord's Prayer with the Jesus Prayer.

## Private worship

- Private prayer is a way of communicating with God on a personal level.
- Many Christians have a rule of regular, daily prayer and Bible reading.
- One form of private prayer is meditation, in which the person praying tries to escape from any distractions to focus entirely on God.
- Another form of private prayer is arrow prayer. Anywhere, at any time, someone may utter a quick prayer such as 'Lord, what should I do now?', 'Lord, please help me.' It is as though the prayer is fired off to God like an arrow from a bow.
- Often private worship is extempore, in the individual's own words.
- Aids to prayer such as a rosary are often used in private prayer.

## Different forms of public worship

Public worship allows Christians to share the experience of worship with others and to support and encourage each other. Different Christian traditions worship in different ways. Note that while for each form of worship a number of traditions are listed which worship in that way, those traditions may sometimes use other forms of worship.

- Liturgical worship is worship following a set form of words and actions. The form of service is contained in books and is followed in many places of worship within the tradition. There are set Bible readings and special prayers to be used at different times of the Christian year. Examples of liturgical worship are the Orthodox **Liturgy** and the Eucharist in the Roman Catholic and Anglican Churches.

- Non-liturgical worship is sometimes structured. There may be a pattern of hymns, Bible readings, **preaching** and prayers which is followed at most services and with which everyone is familiar, even though there is no official set order. The United Reformed Church and Methodist Churches often worship in this way.

- Other non-liturgical worship is spontaneous. There is no structure or set pattern. This worship may be charismatic in style, inspired and led by the Holy Spirit among the worshippers. Hymns, songs and choruses are sung. Readings from the Bible are important in such Spirit-led worship. Another feature is **testimony**, as individuals tell of their own faith and their spiritual experiences, sharing their joy and excitement with everyone there.

- At a Quaker meeting, those present sit around a central table on which is a Bible. They wait in silence for the Holy Spirit. One of those present may feel moved by the Spirit to speak or to read from the Bible.

## Try these short questions

What is meant by

**a** meditation? (2 marks)

**b** extempore prayer? (2 marks)

**c** liturgical worship? (2 marks)

**d** icon? (2 marks)

## Exam-type questions

**a** **i** Name one Christian tradition/denomination in which the kind of worship shown here is the most usual form of worship. (1 mark)

**ii** Describe an act of worship in the tradition you have named. (4 marks)

**b** 'The most important thing about public worship is that it makes the worshippers feel good.' Do you agree? Give reasons for your answer, showing that you have thought about more than one point of view. (5 marks)

(AQA, 2002)

### Student's answer

*a* *i* Pentecostal.

*ii* The worship is very lively. People feel free to express themselves as they wish. They clap and wave their arms in the air to show their excitement and their love of God. The songs are happy ones. There are Bible readings and prayers and someone talks about God and Jesus. When people get very excited they shout 'Alleluia' and 'Praise the Lord'.

6 *I think that worship needs to be brought up to date. If it is boring, no young people will want to know. They will feel fed up and not feel good about it at all. There should be modern hymns that are fun to sing and dance to. Some people might say it is better to have solemn services because they are more religious. I still think that if people do not enjoy the hymns and if they cannot sing and dance as they like they will not bother with church.*

## Examiner's comments

**a** **i** Correct. Mark: 1/1

**ii** This is a fairly good basic description of the worship, with the main aspects covered. 'Someone talks about God and Jesus' is badly expressed. 'Someone speaks about the Christian faith and its relevance to people's lives' would be better. The main weakness is that the response fails to capture the spirit of the worship and becomes a list of things that may happen with no explanation. There is no reference to the power and influence of the Holy Spirit who, they believe, is filling their hearts and inspiring them. Mark: 3/4

**b** The student loses the way and answers a question which is not really there. The response is about what would make worship more attractive to young people. Some credit would be gained because, although it is not directed properly to the question, part of what has been written is relevant. The student has written about the importance of people enjoying worship because if they do not they will find worship difficult or will not worship at all. A full response would deal directly with the purpose of worship, which is not the amusement of the worshipper but an offering to God. Good marks would be gained by, for instance, an argument that a suitable offering of worship to God should come from the heart, and that it can only do so if the worshipper is interested and can join in wholeheartedly. The material used would be much the same, but the approach would be much more effective. Mark: 1/5

## Examination practice

**a** Some Christians use icons to help them in their prayer. Why do they do this? (3 marks)

**b** Some Christians use candles and statues to help them in their prayer. Why do they do this? (4 marks)

**c** Explain how Roman Catholics use rosary beads. (4 marks) (NEAB, 1998)

## Checklist for revision

| | Understand and know | Need more revision | Do not understand |
|---|---|---|---|
| I know what prayer is and why Christians pray. | ☐ | ☐ | ☐ |
| I know what is meant by liturgical and non-liturgical worship and I can give examples of each. | ☐ | ☐ | ☐ |
| I understand the reasons for the use of rosaries, icons and statues. | ☐ | ☐ | ☐ |

# 17 Festivals

## Topic summary

- Many Christians remember significant events, particularly in the life of Jesus, on certain days.
- The festivals are in two groups or cycles.
  - The Christmas cycle, focusing on the birth of Jesus and its significance.
  - The Easter cycle, focusing on the death and resurrection of Jesus and their significance.
- Some Christians mark the festivals with special ceremonies in their worship or other customs. These **observances** stress the Christian message of the festival.

## What do I need to know?

- The festivals are very important in specifications **1A** and **1B**. You should be ready for a question relating to one or more of the following festivals.
- **1A** Advent, Christmas, Epiphany
  Lent, Holy Week, Easter, Pentecost
- **1B** Advent, Christmas, Epiphany
  Lent, Holy Week, Easter, Ascension, Pentecost
- For each festival you need to know the relevant events in the life of Jesus and the early Church, the importance of the festival to Christians, ceremonies and customs used by Christians in their worship and celebrations.

## The Christmas cycle of festivals

### Advent

Advent is the time of preparation for Christmas, beginning on the fourth Sunday before Christmas. During Advent Christians prepare to celebrate the first coming of Jesus, as a child in Bethlehem. They also think of his second coming, remembering that Jesus said that one day he would come again, as a judge at the end of the world.

### Christmas

Christmas (25 December) is the day when Christians celebrate the birth of Jesus Christ, God the Son. Christmas celebrates the Christian belief that the birth of Jesus was unique. A normal human birth is the beginning of the life of a person who, until that person was conceived, simply did not exist. Christians believe that Jesus, the Son of God, has always existed – there was never a time when he did not exist.

Background Bible passages: Luke 2: 1–20; Matthew 1: 18–25; Matthew 2: 1–12; See pages 13–14.

### Epiphany

Epiphany means 'showing'. After Jesus' birth his unique nature was shown to the world. On the day itself, 6 January, after the twelve days of the Christmas season, Christians remember the coming of the Magi, the Wise Men. They are the first recorded visitors to Jesus who were not Jews, members of the race with whom, in the Old Testament, God made a covenant. The Magi symbolize Jesus being shown to people of every nation.

### Christian customs and ceremonies linked with Christmas

Some customs are based on the idea of Jesus being the Light of the World. Light represents truth and goodness, overcoming darkness and evil. A light can be there to lead – people can follow the light.

- Advent rings are used to mark the weeks to Christmas. Often there are four candles on the ring with a fifth, white candle, in the centre. During the first week of Advent one candle is lit, during the second week two candles and so on. During the twelve days of Christmas the central candle is lit as well as the other four.

- Christingle services are very popular during Advent. A Christingle is an orange (representing the world) with a candle (Jesus the Light of the World). Round the orange is a red ribbon (the blood of Jesus shed for the sins of the world) and on four cocktail sticks there are sweets and small fruits (the fruits of the earth).

- A Christmas crib, a model of the stable in which Jesus was born, with figures of the infant Jesus in the manger, Mary and Joseph, the angel Gabriel, the shepherds, Magi, and some animals – ox, donkey and sheep. In some churches the figures are added to the crib at the appropriate times – for example, the Christchild is not added until Christmas Day, the Magi are put in place at Epiphany.

- Carol services are occasions when, by singing familiar carols and hearing readings from the Bible, Christians recall the meaning of the birth of Jesus. Also, carol singers go from house to house or sing in public places, raising money for charity as well as celebrating the Christmas message.

- At Midnight Mass on Christmas Eve the congregation receive Holy Communion at the beginning of Christmas Day.

## The Easter cycle of festivals

### Lent

Lent is the time of preparation for Easter. It begins on Ash Wednesday and lasts six and a half weeks (40 days, not counting Sundays) because Jesus spent 40 days fasting and being tempted. During Lent many Christians pay special attention to their spiritual lives.

- They give up a pleasure (such as sweets, biscuits, alcohol) throughout Lent. Any money saved is given to a Christian charity.
- They give more time to prayer, worship and Bible study.
- They may choose a sin or weakness in their lives (such as swearing or losing their temper) and try to overcome it for good.

The last week of Lent, the week leading up to Easter, is Holy Week, in which fall Palm Sunday, Maundy Thursday (also called Holy Thursday), Good Friday and Holy Saturday.

**beware**

If you give an example of a custom used by Christians at their festivals, make sure it is a custom with a Christian meaning. For example, for Christmas a Christingle would be a good example; the pulling of crackers would not!

## Palm Sunday

Palm Sunday recalls Jesus riding into Jerusalem on a donkey. Centuries before, the prophet Zechariah had foretold that the Messiah would come to Jerusalem riding on a donkey. People greeted him with great excitement, shouting 'Hosanna!' 'Save now.'

At many services on Palm Sunday crosses made from palm leaves are blessed and given to the congregation. The crosses are a reminder that when Jesus rode into Jerusalem he was going there to be crucified. Palm branches may be carried in processions or used to decorate the church.

See Temptation, pages 19–20.

## Maundy Thursday

Maundy Thursday marks the day of the Last Supper, which Jesus shared with his disciples. Jesus gave his disciples bread and wine with the words 'This is my Body', 'This is my Blood' (see the Eucharist, pages 62–5). He also gave them a new commandment – 'Love one another.' To show his disciples an example of loving and serving others, Jesus washed his disciples' feet. This was a task for a slave or servant. Jesus said to his disciples, 'Now that I, your Lord and Teacher, have washed your feet, you also should wash one another's feet. I have set you an example that you should do as I have done for you.'

Mark 11: 1–11; see page 19.

Many churches have communion services on Maundy Thursday. At some, the priest may wash the feet of some of the congregation as a symbol of the action of Jesus and a reminder of his command to love one another.

Mark 14: 22–5; John 13: 1–15; John 13: 34–5.

## Good Friday

Good Friday marks the day of the crucifixion. According to the Gospels, Jesus died at 3 pm. His body was taken to a tomb in a garden belonging to Joseph of Arimathaea. Some women who were followers of Jesus started to prepare his body for burial.

See the section on the suffering and death of Jesus, pages 23–7

In many towns and cities there are processions of witness with one or two people at the front of the procession carrying a large cross. In some churches there are services, lasting between one and three hours, timed to end at 3pm. These services focus on the accounts of the crucifixion in the Gospels. One feature is often the bringing of a large wooden cross, which worshippers kiss as an act of reverence.

The evening service in Orthodox churches recalls the burial of Jesus. An icon of the dead Christ, wrapped in burial clothes, is brought into the church. Worshippers show their devotion by kissing the icon.

## Holy Saturday

Saturday is the Sabbath, the Jewish day of rest. Since no work is done on the Sabbath, the women did not return to complete the burial **rites**. The body of Jesus was left in the tomb.

**did you know?** When Christians talk about witness they mean saying and doing things to show what they believe.

## Easter Day

At some point during the night between the Saturday and the Sunday, Jesus rose from the dead. No one witnessed the resurrection. When the women came to the tomb on the Sunday they found it empty. Later, Jesus was seen by many of his followers.

Easter Vigil services, marking the resurrection, take place during the hours of darkness, either on the Saturday evening or early on the Sunday morning. The whole church is in darkness. At the main door of the church a light is struck – the New Fire of Easter. The Paschal candle (Easter candle), representing the risen Jesus, is lit. The candle is marked with various symbols of Jesus. It is carried in procession through the church to a special candlestick, which will stand in a prominent place throughout the Easter season. The congregation have small hand-candles, which they light from the Paschal candle as it passes them. The resurrection light spreads round the church just as the Gospel news of the resurrection spread round the world.

See the section on the resurrection of Jesus, pages 30–2.

## Ascension 1B

Forty days after Jesus rose from death he left the world to return to heaven, to God the Father. Note that the emphasis here is not so much on the end of Jesus' time on earth as on his triumphant return to reign in glory in heaven again.

Christians believe that Jesus is God the Son and that, before his time on earth, he had always been with the Father. He is God; his nature is divine. When he was born in Bethlehem, he took human nature. When he returned to heaven, he returned as both divine and human. Heaven was opened to human beings at the Ascension.

Acts 1: 1–11

Christians believe that Jesus is ever in heaven, praying for every human being. When Christians pray, they join their prayers with the prayer of Jesus. That is why Christians often end prayers with words such as 'through Jesus Christ our Lord'.

## Pentecost

Pentecost (Whitsun) celebrates the coming of the Holy Spirit to the followers of Jesus. Jesus had told them to wait until the Spirit came to them. Ten days after the Ascension, 50 days after the resurrection, the Spirit came.

Their experience of the Spirit sounds strange. They heard a great wind, flames of fire appeared on their heads. The most important thing was that they felt the power of the Spirit in them. From now on they were apostles – they had a God-given message and they had to make it known. Pentecost marked the beginning of the Church.

Christians in some towns and cities in the north of England have traditionally taken part in Whit Walks. Christians from many denominations walk in procession through the streets. Hundreds of people turn out to watch them. The Whit Walks are acts of witness. As the apostles preached the Gospel in words, so the walkers show their faith by marching through the town.

Acts 2 describes what happened when the Holy Spirit came to the apostles.

# Why do Christians celebrate festivals?

- Festivals recall the key events in the life of Jesus and the Church. Christians are able to focus on those events and their meaning.
- Christians celebrate together at the festivals. The celebrations are a bond between them.
- Some festivals, Christmas and Easter in particular, have a high profile. At these times, Christians have an opportunity to witness to their beliefs and make others aware of the meaning of the events they are celebrating.
- Some festivals, such as Epiphany and Ascension, pass unnoticed by most people. These festivals still allow Christians to focus on important aspects of their faith.

**did you know?** Some Christians do not celebrate the festivals. Others only celebrate the main ones.

## Try these short questions

**a i** On what day do Christians celebrate the birth of Jesus? (1 mark)

**ii** Why is that event important to Christians? (2 marks)

**b i** What event in the life of Jesus do Christians remember on Good Friday? (1 mark)

**ii** Why is that event important to Christians? (2 marks)

**c i** What event in the life of Jesus do Christians remember on Easter Day? (1 mark)

**ii** Why is that event important to Christians? (2 marks)

**d i** On what day do Christians celebrate the coming of the Holy Spirit to the apostles? (1 mark)

**ii** Why is that event important to Christians? (2 marks)

## Exam-type questions

**a** Explain what is happening in the drawing. (2 marks)

**b** Why is Ash Wednesday important to Christians? (4 marks)

**c** 'Ceremonies like the one in the drawing are old-fashioned and have no meaning today.' Do you agree? Give reasons for your answers, showing that you have thought about more than one point of view. (5 marks)

(NEAB, 2001)

### Student's answer

*a The priest is making the sign of the cross on the person's forehead because it is Ash Wednesday.*

*b Ash Wednesday is important to Christians because it is the beginning of Lent. Lent is the time when Jesus was in the wilderness for 40 days and 40 nights. Christians give things up for Lent – things like sweets and cigarettes.*

*c I agree and I do not agree. The ceremony with the ash is old-fashioned because it has been going on for years. But I can see the point of it. When you are baptized you are cleansed from sin. The priest makes the sign of the cross on your forehead. On Ash Wednesday he makes the sign again but this time with ash, to show you have sinned. Also, if you go to church and have an ash cross and leave it there all day it shows you are a Christian and the day is important.*

## Examiner's comments

**a** The student has said what happens but has not said why. Add 'It shows people are sorry they have sinned' or 'The priest uses words like *Turn away from sin and believe the good news*'. The fact that some material, which is relevant here, is used does not help the student at this point. The meaning of the ash cross is known, but students are assessed partly on their skill in selecting the right material in the right context.    Mark: 1/2

**b** A number of statements are made, all true and relevant, but the main point is missed. Lent is the time of preparation for Easter, the greatest festival of the Christian Year. The reason for giving up pleasures is that self-discipline is seen as a way of focusing more strongly on spiritual matters. Christians offer their self-control to God. Also, though the student knows about Jesus being in the wilderness for 40 days and nights, there is no hint of why he was there or why this is important to Christians.    Mark: 2/4

**c** The student makes an effort to consider both sides of the question but in fact only discusses one – the argument against. The ceremony is presented as relevant to a Christian's spiritual experience and is also seen as an act of witness – it can take courage to be seen to have been marked with ash. It could be argued that there is nothing wrong with an old tradition; keeping up traditions might be seen as a good thing. On the other hand, students could argue that Christianity is not about outward signs but about the way Christians live their lives, loving God and their neighbour. Dirty marks on the forehead seem strange and meaningless to many people.    Mark: 3/5

## Examination practice

**a** Describe and explain two ceremonies or customs which are used in Christian worship during Advent and/or Christmas to show why the birth of Jesus is important to Christians. (10 marks)

**b** Do you think Christians can use the way they celebrate Christmas to show other people how important their faith is to them? Give reasons for your answer, showing that you have thought about more than one point of view. (5 marks)    (NEAB, 1999)

# Checklist for revision

| | Understand and know | Need more revision | Do not understand |
|---|---|---|---|
| I know why Advent, Christmas and Epiphany are important to Christians. | ☐ | ☐ | ☐ |
| I can describe and explain two Christian ceremonies or customs linked with Advent, Christmas and Epiphany. | ☐ | ☐ | ☐ |
| I know why Lent, Holy Week and Easter are important to Christians. | ☐ | ☐ | ☐ |
| I can describe and explain ways in which Christians observe Lent. | ☐ | ☐ | ☐ |
| I can describe and explain a Christian ceremony or custom linked with each significant day in Holy Week. | ☐ | ☐ | ☐ |
| I can describe and explain ways in which Christians observe Easter. | ☐ | ☐ | ☐ |
| 1B  I know why Ascension is important to Christians. | ☐ | ☐ | ☐ |
| I know why Pentecost is important to Christians. | ☐ | ☐ | ☐ |

# 18 Abortion

## Topic summary

- Christians believe that life is sacred. Some believe that life begins at conception and therefore **abortion** is murder. Other Christians believe that there may be difficult circumstances where abortion is permissible.
- Abortion is permitted in this country by the Human Fertilization and Embryology Act 1990. The Act outlines situations in which a woman can request and be given an abortion.
- Various passages in the Bible stress the uniqueness of human life in God's **creation**.

## What do I need to know?

- Differing viewpoints on abortion, including relevant medical and social issues.
- Attitudes of Christians towards abortion. **2B** Special emphasis on Roman Catholic teaching.
- Relevant Bible passages which are part of your course.
  Genesis 1: 26–7; Exodus 20: 1–17; 1 Corinthians 6: 18–20

## The Abortion Acts, 1967 and 1990

It was once illegal to have an abortion in the United Kingdom. Women who wanted an abortion had to find secret, illegal ways of terminating their pregnancies. Women who could not afford a private clinic could either go to 'back street' clinics, often staffed by unqualified or under-qualified people, or try to terminate their pregnancies at home, using such things as knitting needles and alcohol.

In both cases, many women died from infection or haemorrhaging. Others became seriously ill and, in some cases, unable to have more children in the future.

The 1967 Abortion Act allowed women to seek an abortion in all areas of the United Kingdom, except Northern Ireland. Two doctors must agree that if the pregnancy continues there is:

- risk of injury to the physical or mental health of the pregnant woman
- risk of injury to the physical or mental health of any existing children of the pregnant woman
- risk to the life of the pregnant woman
- a real risk that the child would suffer from such physical or mental disabilities as to be seriously handicapped.

The Abortion Act was amended by the Human Fertilization and Embryology Act 1990. Great medical advances had occurred since 1967. In some cases, premature babies are now able to survive outside the womb after 24 weeks. The 1990 Act stated that abortions should only take place up to the 24th week of pregnancy. Abortions

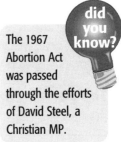

**did you know?**

The 1967 Abortion Act was passed through the efforts of David Steel, a Christian MP.

performed after that point are very rare, usually in cases where the mother's life is in danger. Many take place before the foetus is twelve weeks old.

# When does human life begin?

People's opinions on the rights and wrongs of abortion are based to an extent on when they believe human life begins.

- Some people believe that human life begins at the moment of conception, when the fertilized egg attaches itself to the wall of the womb.
- Others believe that human life begins at the point when the human embryo becomes a foetus in the womb, at about eight weeks.
- Others believe that human life begins when a baby can live outside its mother's womb. Until that point, they say that the baby is part of the mother's body.

Many believe that abortion is always wrong as it kills a human being. Others say that a pregnant woman has the right to decide what happens to a part of her body.

# What do the Churches say about abortion?

All Christian Churches state that human life is special and God-given.

## *The Anglican viewpoint*

The Anglican **Church** teaches that abortion is wrong, especially when used as a means of birth control. The foetus in the womb should be protected and nurtured as a gift from God. However, it accepts that in a few circumstances abortion may be a merciful option, for example, in cases of rape or if the mother's life is in danger.

The Anglican General Synod of 1983 made the following statement about abortion:

> 'The Church of England combines strong opposition to abortion with the recognition that there can be strictly limited conditions under which it may be morally preferable to any alternative.'

## *The Roman Catholic viewpoint*

The Roman Catholic Church teaches that human life begins at the moment of conception. Therefore abortion is murder at any stage of the foetus' development. The life of the child in the womb is sacred and God-given; to end that life through abortion is never acceptable. Instead, support and pastoral care should be given to those facing parenthood in difficult circumstances.

The Second Vatican Council (1962–5) stated that, 'Life must be protected with the utmost care from the moment of conception: abortion and infanticide are abominable crimes.'

# The views of other organizations

There are a large number of organizations who campaign both for and against the abortion issue. They can be divided into two main groups.

**1.** Pro-life

- *LIFE* – the members of this organization believe that all human life should be protected by the law. An unwanted or severely handicapped child has as much right to life as any other child.

**did you know?**

In the United Kingdom, the father of the foetus has no right to prevent an abortion. The decision whether to have an abortion or not rests solely on the mother.

- *The Society for the Protection of Unborn Children (SPUC)* not only opposes abortion but also provides educational material and support for women and, with other pro-life groups, campaigns to bring pro-life issues to the attention of national and international governments.

**2.** Pro-choice

- *The National Abortion Campaign (NAC)* promotes the slogan 'Our bodies, our lives, our right to decide.' This group believes that whether or not a woman wants to continue with her pregnancy or to terminate it, she has the right to make the best decision for herself. She should always be given an informed choice. The NAC provides contraception and abortion advice.

- *Marie Stopes International* – this organization's mission is to 'ensure the fundamental human right of all people to have children by choice not chance'. It offers abortion services and also provides care for women who decide to continue their pregnancies in difficult circumstances.

# Arguments for and against abortion

## The case for abortion (Pro-choice)

- If abortion were illegal, many women would still risk their lives in back street clinics and at home.
- A woman has the right to choose what is best for her and her family. As long as she seeks professional advice, she is best placed to make the decision.
- If a woman is raped and becomes pregnant, or if she discovers that her unborn child is severely handicapped, an abortion is a humane option.
- Abortion prevents children from growing up knowing they are unwanted.
- Many areas of the world are over-populated. Women, particularly in poorer parts of the world, should have ready access to contraception and abortion for the sake of their existing children.
- If a woman's life is at risk during the pregnancy, many would argue that her life, rather than the foetus', should be saved. She may have dependants and responsibilities – the unborn child does not.

## The case against abortion (Pro-life)

- Many Christians believe that human life begins at conception. A child is a gift from God and part of his creation. Abortion, for any reason, is murder.
- Although a foetus cannot argue for itself, it has the right to live. Society should protect those who cannot protect themselves.
- Unborn babies have enormous potential. What right has anyone to deny the difference that a child might make to the world?
- Babies born with severe handicaps often grow up to lead fulfilled lives.
- A foetus is a living, feeling being. Some doctors claim, through their research, that an aborted foetus experiences great pain before death.
- Many women experience guilt after their unborn child has been aborted. This may affect them for the rest of their lives.
- If abortion is acceptable, where do we draw the line? Which members of society, considered to be unwanted, are next?

> **hints and tips**
>
> In the exam you may be asked to give arguments for and against the abortion issue. Make sure that you can give several arguments on both sides, backed up by passages from the Bible.

# What are the alternatives to abortion?

● During and after her pregnancy, the woman can seek support from Christian organizations, pro-life groups and Social Services.

● The baby, once born, can be given up for adoption. Couples who are unable to have children frequently adopt a child and bring it up as their own.

● The baby can be fostered giving the mother time to change her mind if her circumstances change. If not, the child can be put forward for adoption later.

● Young, single mothers often discover that their own families are willing to offer support, guidance and care for mother and child within the family home.

# Relevant Bible passages

In this section you will find the three Bible passages specified by your exam board for the topics on abortion and **voluntary euthanasia** (see pages 104–7).

### Genesis 1: 26–7

This passage shows the unique place human beings have in God's creation. We are created in his image, somehow to be like him. Human life is precious and special to God; it should be protected particularly at its most vulnerable stages – the beginning and end of life.

### Exodus 20: 1–17

The Ten **Commandments** were given by God as a pattern for good and moral living. Many Christians believe that the commandment, 'You shall not murder', supports the view that abortion and voluntary euthanasia are wrong and against the will of God. Both are seen as murder.

### 1 Corinthians 6: 19–20

In his letter to the people of Corinth, Paul says that God's Spirit is present in our bodies. We must treat our bodies with the greatest respect and protect them from harm as God lives within us.

> read more
>
> Psalm 139: 13–16;
> Jeremiah 1: 5;
> Luke 12: 4–7

## Try these short questions

a   Explain the term 'abortion'. (2 marks)

b   State two options a Christian may choose instead of abortion. (2 marks)

(NEAB, 2000)

## Exam-type questions

Some Christians will agree with abortion in certain circumstances; other Christians say that abortion is always wrong. Using your knowledge of Christian teaching, explain how each group might justify its own position. (5 marks)                                             (SEG, 1998)

## Student's answer

Some Christians would say that abortion is acceptable if the pregnancy is the result of rape. Christians believe that God is a God of love. He would not want a woman to suffer by carrying and giving birth to a child who had been forced on her. The child would always remind her of her terrible experience. Also, what if a woman was in danger of dying because of her pregnancy? If she was married and had children, they would lose a wife and mother. Jesus said that we must 'love our neighbours as ourselves'. Some Christians think that saying that these two women cannot have an abortion is not showing love.

Other Christians, for example Roman Catholics, believe that abortion is always wrong whatever the situation. They say that abortion is murder. They also say that it goes against the commandment, 'You shall not kill.' These Christians also believe that life begins at conception and is placed there by God. When He created the world, God made humans in His own image – we are special! Psalm 139 tells us that God knows and loves everyone even in the womb. He may have a special purpose for us. How can a baby be aborted just because it is inconvenient?

## Examiner's comments

This is a very good answer. Notice that the student has given two examples of situations where Christians may think abortion is acceptable. The student has referred to the Christian teaching of a God of love and has included Jesus' teaching on loving one another. The student has also shown why abortion is never acceptable to some Christians and has given an example of a **tradition** which believes this. Again, two passages from the Bible have been correctly used to back up this opinion. A well-balanced answer.

Mark: 5/5

## Examination practice

'I'm 39, married and pregnant. Tests show that our unborn baby is severely disabled. I'm going to have an abortion.' Explain **one** Christian reply to this woman. (3 marks)   (AQA, 2002)

# Checklist for revision

| | Understand and know | Need more revision | Do not understand |
|---|---|---|---|
| I can explain the term 'abortion'. | ☐ | ☐ | ☐ |
| I can give at least three alternatives to abortion. | ☐ | ☐ | ☐ |
| I can explain why many Christians are against abortion. | ☐ | ☐ | ☐ |
| I can give the views of organizations who are both for and against abortion. | ☐ | ☐ | ☐ |
| I can refer to and explain at least three relevant passages from the Bible on this topic. | ☐ | ☐ | ☐ |

# 19 Voluntary euthanasia

## Topic summary

- All Christians believe that life is sacred and that the taking away of life is wrong. It is against the will of God who gives life. Some Christians believe that abortion and voluntary euthanasia go against the commandment, 'You shall not murder.' Other Christians believe that there may be difficult circumstances where abortion and voluntary euthanasia are merciful options.
- Voluntary euthanasia is currently against the law in the United Kingdom and is classed as a criminal act.
- Various passages in the Bible stress the uniqueness of human life in God's creation. They teach that life is a gift from God and that each life is precious to him.

## What do I need to know?

- What is meant by voluntary euthanasia.
- Differing attitudes to voluntary euthanasia, with particular emphasis on Christian viewpoints **2B** stressing Roman Catholic teaching.
- Relevant Bible teaching concerning the sacredness of life.

**read more**
The passages are the same as those relating to abortion, see page 102.

Euthanasia is the practice of helping people who are seriously ill and in intolerable pain to die, either at their own request or by others deciding to take away life support.

Your specification requires you to understand the meaning of, and issues surrounding voluntary euthanasia. This is where a person suffering from an incurable disease or injury asks help from a doctor, relative or friend to die with dignity. Other names for voluntary euthanasia include assisted suicide, mercy killing, and easy or gentle death.

People, including Christians, are divided on the issue of voluntary euthanasia.

- Some people feel that a patient in these circumstances should be allowed to seek help to die, provided that they are lucid and understand the seriousness of their request. They believe that voluntary euthanasia will remove their suffering and may help to ease the suffering of family and friends.
- Others believe that assisting someone to die is fundamentally wrong. It goes against the commandment, 'You shall not murder.' Christians believe that human beings are God's creation and made in his image. Many say that people have a duty to help those who suffer, but that they must not commit murder. Is it not 'playing God' to decide when a person should die?

**did you know?**
At their graduation ceremony, many doctors take the ancient Hippocratic Oath. They solemnly promise that they will do no harm. They also say that they 'will exercise their art solely for the cure of patients and will give no drug for a criminal purpose, even if solicited'.

Currently, voluntary euthanasia is illegal in the United Kingdom and those who help others to die risk being charged as an accessory to murder.

# What do the Churches say about voluntary euthanasia?

## The Roman Catholic viewpoint

The Roman Catholic Church condemns voluntary euthanasia. As God gives life and life is sacred, only he can make the decision as to when that life should end. Special care and support should be given to the person to help them approach death in peace. In its 'Declaration on Euthanasia, 1980', the Roman Catholic Church stated that doctors, when faced with a terminally ill patient, 'should not give anything with the deliberate intention of killing the patient.'

On the other hand, Roman Catholics accept that pain-killing drugs may quicken death. This is seen as a side effect; the illness or injury has ended the person's life.

## The Anglican viewpoint

As human life is a gift from God to be protected and cherished, the Anglican Church teaches that deliberate taking of life is wrong and is opposed to voluntary euthanasia.

The Anglican Church does not insist that a dying or seriously ill patient should be kept alive by medical treatment and technology indefinitely. There is a great difference between withdrawing treatment during the last days of a terminal illness, when it probably would not help anyway, and giving a lethal injection at a patient's request. The patient has the right to refuse treatment, but not the right to die when they choose.

## The Methodist viewpoint

The Methodist Church states that more time and resources should be given to providing better care and facilities for those facing terminal illness.

> 'The argument for euthanasia will be answered if better methods of caring for the dying can be developed. Medical skill in terminal care must be improved. The whole of the patient's needs, including the spiritual, must be met.'
>
> (Methodist Church, 1974)

# The views of other organizations

- *EXIT* campaigns for a change in the law; its members believe that voluntary euthanasia should be legalized. They believe that a terminally ill patient should have the right to request a peaceful end to their suffering.
- *The Voluntary Euthanasia Society* believes that people should have the right to request death if life has become unbearable through illness or injury. They also recommend the writing of a 'living will'. Individuals state which treatments they would or would not want should they become seriously ill in the future and unable to express their wishes.

# The case for and against voluntary euthanasia

## The case for voluntary euthanasia

- Those who are terminally ill or very seriously injured are often in tremendous pain. Helping them to die, if that is their wish, will end their suffering. Their families will also be spared the anguish of watching a loved one's slow, painful death.

- They may wish to die with dignity before they become too ill to look after themselves and a burden on their family and friends.

- Jesus showed compassion to the sick and dying and voluntary euthanasia is compassionate. He taught that his followers should 'love their neighbour as themselves'. Some people would say that helping someone, who has no quality of life and no hope of recovery, to die is showing love.

- Others would argue that much loved pets are gently 'put to sleep' when their suffering becomes too great. If this mercy can be shown to animals, why cannot human beings be granted the same?

### The case against voluntary euthanasia

- Many Christians say that voluntary euthanasia goes against the commandment 'You shall not murder'. Life is a gift from God. Only God has the right to take life away.

- Medical advances are happening all the time. A cure may be found for a person's condition.

- Some Christians believe that suffering strengthens **faith** and brings a person closer to God. Many believe that **miracles** happen through the power of faith and **prayer**.

- Would it always be possible to be absolutely certain that a document signed by a patient was really what the patient wanted? What if the patient had a change of heart and was not well enough to express it? Was the patient thinking clearly when the document was signed?

- It is a doctor's duty to save life, not destroy it. Should we expect doctors to live with the consequences of voluntary euthanasia if it is legalized?

- Many Christians believe that voluntary euthanasia is potentially dangerous to society. If it is acceptable, where do we draw the line? Some fear that human life will be less valued.

**beware**

In the exam, if you refer to a patient on life support, in a coma or relatives deciding to switch off the machine, this is referring to involuntary euthanasia. This is not relevant for questions about voluntary euthanasia and will gain you no marks.

## What are the alternatives to voluntary euthanasia?

- Painkillers – modern painkillers are more effective and do not have as many serious side effects. They help control the level of pain.

- Hospices – these are special hospitals for the terminally ill. The Hospice Movement originated from the concern of Christians that people should be allowed to die with dignity in a caring and specialized environment. People of all religions and of no religion are welcome at hospices. Hospices also provide respite care for the families of the terminally ill. Counsellors and chaplains help the patient to prepare for death and assist the family in the grieving process.

- Many Christians look to their Church communities for support. Priests and ministers help the person to prepare for death. Christians find great comfort in the knowledge that others are praying for them and with them.

- Alternative medicines and therapy are becoming more popular. Some people find that yoga, acupuncture and homeopathic remedies relieve pain, help relaxation and give peace of mind.

## Try these short questions

**a** Explain the term 'voluntary euthanasia' (2 marks)

**b** Give a reason Christians might give both for and against voluntary euthanasia. Give **one** reason in each case. (4 marks)

## Exam-type questions

Explain **two** situations in which some Christians think that euthanasia is acceptable. (4 marks)

(NEAB, 1999)

### Student's answer

Many Christians are against euthanasia as they think that God created us and only he can make decisions about death. But some Christians think that euthanasia is acceptable in some cases. For example, if a person is permanently disabled he may be in terrible pain. The doctors cannot heal him and he cannot look after himself. He has no dignity. Jesus tried to help those who were suffering. Voluntary euthanasia could be said to show mercy and love to people who cannot stand the suffering anymore.

Also, euthanasia means 'easy, gentle death'. A person with a terminal illness is already dying. Euthanasia can be used to help death come a little quicker, perhaps at home surrounded by loved ones.

### Examiner's comments

The first part of this answer is quite good. The student has stated that euthanasia is not acceptable to many Christians and then goes on to show that, in some circumstances, it may be acceptable to other Christians. The first situation gives a concrete example of where euthanasia may be acceptable. The second part of the answer, whilst giving a further example, is weak. Terminally ill patients already have the right to die at home surrounded by loved ones if they wish, without euthanasia. Notice, also, that the student has made no reference to Christian teaching or a relevant passage from the Bible. There is a brief reference to the fact that Jesus helped those who were suffering – a rather vague comment.

Mark: 2/4

## Examination practice

What passage from the Bible might a Christian quote **either** in support of **or** against voluntary euthanasia? (4 marks)

## Checklist for revision

| | Understand and know | Need more revision | Do not understand |
|---|---|---|---|
| I can explain the term 'voluntary euthanasia'. | ☐ | ☐ | ☐ |
| I can give at least three alternatives to voluntary euthanasia. | ☐ | ☐ | ☐ |
| I can give the views of Christians for and against voluntary euthanasia. | ☐ | ☐ | ☐ |
| I can refer to and explain at least three relevant passages from the Bible. | ☐ | ☐ | ☐ |

## Topic summary

- Many Christians believe in the Bible's account of the creation of the world by God. Others believe that today's world is the result of a gradual **evolution** over millions of years and that God's work can be seen in evolution.
- Whatever their beliefs, many feel that it is each generation's duty to protect the world and leave it in a good condition for their children.
- However, there is strong evidence that the balance of nature is being affected by our lifestyles, industries and carelessness.
- In recent years, international organizations have appealed to the governments of the world and to individuals to become better stewards of the planet before the damage goes too far.

## What do I need to know?

- Christian beliefs about the creation of the world by God.
- The theory of evolution.
- The idea of humanity's stewardship of the world.
- Examples of the ways in which modern living is damaging the **environment**.
- What can be done to put things right?
- Passages from the Bible related to this topic. Genesis 1–2: 3

## The biblical account of creation

> God saw all that he had made and it was very good. (Genesis 1: 31)

The account of creation can be found in the opening two chapters of Genesis, the first book of the Bible. These chapters describe how, in six days, God created the world and all living things from a formless and empty darkness.

According to Genesis 2: 15, 19–20, God placed humanity on the earth to work the land and take care of it. There seems to be a special relationship between human beings and all other living creatures in that God brings them all to Adam to be named by him. In a sense, human beings were to be God's deputies on earth, with a particular responsibility of care and protection.

On the Creation read Genesis 1 and 2

## The theory of evolution

One of the characteristics of scientists is to ask questions. Some of the most sought after answers are to the questions, 'How was the earth formed?' and 'How did life begin?' Scientists' studies have led them to suggest that millions of years ago there was a cosmic explosion which hurled matter in all directions. Simply put, this 'Big Bang' led over millions of years to the formation of the universe and to the planet earth.

**beware**

According to the Bible, God created the world in six days, *not* seven. He rested on the seventh day.

Through the discovery of fossils, many scientists believe that all existing animals, insects and plants have developed by a process of gradual change. Rather than a single, special creation by God, in which every species was made in an unchangeable form, some scientists claim that life began in a very simple form. Gradually, over millions of years, this simple life evolved into many different species. Each species adapted and developed to suit the changing environment. Many scientists believe that all life continues to evolve.

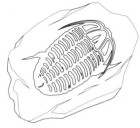

*Many scientists believe that fossils prove that living beings have evolved slowly over millions of years.*

## Can science and Christianity agree?

Some Christians are fundamentalist: they believe that everything in the Bible is true and **inspired** by God. They believe that God created the world and all living beings over six periods of time. Some Christians would claim that, if you studied the account of creation in Genesis 1 alongside the scientific view of how life evolved, you would see a remarkable similarity in the order of events. Other Christians accept the scientific version whilst still seeing God's hand at work in evolution. They believe in a Creator God who is still at work in the evolving world.

In the Apostles' **Creed**, the statement of Christian beliefs, Christians say, 'I believe in God, the Father almighty, creator of heaven and earth.' Whether they are fundamentalist or see God at work in evolution, Christians believe that God is the creator of all life and that humanity is the crown of his creation.

## Humanity's stewardship of the world

Christians believe that the universe owes its continuing existence to God. They believe that he gave humans stewardship of the world, to care for his creation in his place.

Stewardship means to manage or look after something belonging to another. For this topic, this means looking after the world for God and for future generations.

> God blessed them and said to them, 'Be fruitful and increase in number;
> fill the earth and subdue it. Rule over the fish of the sea and the birds of
> the air and over every living creature that moves on the ground.'
>
> (Genesis 1: 28)

Many believe that human beings have not been good stewards of the world. Sadly, those who are concerned seem to be outnumbered by those who show no care.

## Examples of damage

- The Greenhouse Effect – energy from the sun gives rise to the earth's climate and weather. At the same time, the earth radiates energy back into space. Greenhouse gases trap some of this energy, keeping in the heat like the glass panels of a greenhouse. This is good, for without it temperatures on earth would be much lower than they are. The problem is that these gases have become more concentrated due to such things as car fumes, industrial production, fumes from the fuels which heat our houses and CFC's, including aerosol sprays.

- This has led to a serious **pollution** of the world's atmosphere. There is a delicate layer above the earth which protects the world from some of the damaging effects of the sun called the ozone layer. Scientists have seen holes in the ozone layer and this has led to a sharp increase in cases of skin cancer.

- Increased greenhouse gases have led to global warming. Ice caps around the world have started to melt and this causes sea levels to rise. Rivers are overflowing and many areas are experiencing severe flooding.

- Large areas of rainforest have been destroyed. Forests supply the earth with oxygen and yet the trees continue to be chopped down.

- Many of our industries release chemicals into the air and this leads to acid rain. When the acid rain falls, vegetation and river life die.

- Human beings are destroying the natural habitat of many species. This has led to many species becoming extinct and many others are in danger of **extinction**.

- Natural fuels, such as gas, oil and coal, are being wasted. What will replace them when they have gone?

## What can be done to put things right?

It would be so easy to say, 'This is a problem on a worldwide scale. There is nothing that I, as an individual, can do to make a difference!' But if enough individuals did something a difference could be made. Also, individuals can form groups who can bring about greater change and can, in turn, put pressure on the governments of the world.

Individuals can

- stop dropping litter
- stop using aerosols and other forms of CFC's
- use detergents that do not harm the environment
- recycle household waste such as newspapers, plastics, metal and glass
- find other forms of energy to light and warm their homes, for example, solar energy
- use their car less often
- write to their local MP to encourage national and international action.

Groups can

- clean up local areas and rid them of litter and waste
- make a real impact around the world in protecting endangered animals and environments with the force of numbers and finance
- put pressure on their governments to bring about change.

Major voluntary organizations, such as CAFOD, Christian Aid, Tearfund and Trocaire, are involved in environmental issues. For example, they help people in **developing countries** find new methods of farming which prevent soil erosion.

Governments can

- enforce laws in their country to protect the environment
- join with other governments to find ways of halting the damage.

**hints and tips**

In the exam you might be asked to give examples of ways in which young people can help the local environment. Find out what is going on in your area.

## Relevant Bible passages

The main set passage for this topic is Genesis 1–2: 3. This describes the creation of the universe by God in six days. The beauty and perfection of the created world is emphasized at the end of each day of creation, when God looked at the work of the day and 'saw that it was good'.

In this passage, God gives stewardship of the world to humans (see Genesis 1: 28). It is their responsibility to control, cultivate and care for the world. There is also the implication that, as stewards, humans should be able to keep the world in its original perfect condition.

> **read more**
>
> You may find these passages useful for adding weight to the points you make in your answers:
> Deuteronomy 20: 19–20; Psalm 8: 3–8; Psalm 104

### Try these short questions

Cartoon: © Tearfund

**a** How does this cartoon sum up the attitude of some people today? (2 marks)

**b** Choose **one** passage from the Bible which teaches about caring for the environment and

   **i** state what it teaches (2 marks)

   **ii** explain how a Christian might put the teaching of this passage into practice. (3 marks)     (NEAB, 1996)

## Exam-type questions

A young person says, 'The world is in such a mess and I can see the harm we are doing to the planet. But I'm only one person – what can I do? Nobody seems to care.' Do you agree? Give reasons for your answer. (7 marks)

### Student's answer

The young person is right – the world is in a mess! The climate is changing, the ozone layer is damaged, the rainforests are being destroyed and many types of animals are now extinct. Pollution is spoiling everything. All this is because of our greed and lack of care. We live in a throw-away society. One day, if we are not careful, we will throw away our world!

But I do not agree that one person cannot make a difference and that nobody cares. If we all thought like that, nothing would ever get done. There are groups and organizations around the world who work hard to protect the environment and persuade governments to put things right. For example, Greenpeace, CAFOD and Christian Aid.

As a young person, there are many things I can do to help the environment. I can stop dropping litter and encourage my friends to do the same. I can make sure my family uses recycling bins. I can suggest that my family walks more often or uses public transport, rather than jumping into the car all the time. I can join a local youth group which is tidying up a plot of wasteland.

There is so much an individual can do. The young person's attitude will get us nowhere!

### Examiner's comments

This is the type of question you might find in Part C of the exam paper. For 7 marks you need to give quite a lengthy answer. The question, read carefully, falls into three parts: the harm we are doing to the planet, an individual's role in helping the environment and the suggestion that nobody cares.

The candidate has given a good answer. The three parts of the question have been tackled. The candidate has given examples of environmental damage, shown that groups are concerned with environmental issues and has given examples of how an individual can make a difference.

The only point the candidate has missed out is a bible passage. Wherever possible, answers should include a reference to a relevant passage from the Bible. Failure to do so cost this student two marks, even though the response is otherwise a strong one.

In this case, the candidate could have mentioned Genesis 1 and discussed humanity's responsibility as stewards of God's creation.

Mark: 5/7

### Examination practice

The environment in which human beings live includes the air, the land, water, plants and animals. Explain the Christian beliefs about human responsibility for the *whole* environment. (5 marks)

(SEG, 1998)

# Checklist for revision

| | Understand and know | Need more revision | Do not understand |
|---|---|---|---|
| I know what is meant by the terms 'creation' and 'evolution'. | ☐ | ☐ | ☐ |
| I can give at least four examples of ways in which the world is being damaged. | ☐ | ☐ | ☐ |
| I can give examples of how individuals, groups and governments can help with conservation. | ☐ | ☐ | ☐ |
| I can give three examples of relevant Bible passages. | ☐ | ☐ | ☐ |

# 21 Conflict, war and peace

## Topic summary

The basic issue is whether any form of violence is ever right. The answer to the question depends on where you are coming from.

- War may prevent or end something that is evil. On the other hand, war leads to terrible destruction and suffering.
- Some people believe there are things which are so evil that anything which gets rid of those things is justified – even the death of innocent people. They call themselves 'freedom fighters'. Other people call them **terrorists**.
- People have a right to protest against things that they believe are wrong. Some believe that if the cause is just then even violent protest is justified.
- Some people believe that war and violence are never justified, whatever the circumstances. Protest must be non-violent.

## What do I need to know?

- The beliefs of **pacifists** and examples of non-violent protest.
- The idea of a **just war**.
- The meaning of 'freedom fighter', 'terrorist' and 'terrorism'.
- About nuclear war and disarmament.
- The teaching of Jesus.
- Relevant Bible passages.
    - **2A** Matthew 26: 47–53; Mark 11: 15–18; Luke 4: 16–21; Romans 13: 1–7
    - **2B** Exodus 20: 1–17; Matthew 5: 1–12; Matthew 5: 38–48

## Pacifism

In an ideal world everyone would live together in peace. There would be peace in every family, every community, every nation. All countries would work together for the good of the whole human race. Sadly, human nature is not like that.

Coventry Cathedral was destroyed during World War II. The new cathedral was designed to symbolize life triumphing over death and peace over conflict. In the cathedral there is the Chapel of Unity where a black cross hangs over the altar. The community of the cathedral longed for the time when there would be no more war. They promised that when a time came when there was no conflict in the world the cross would be painted white. It is still black.

Pacifists believe in peace. They know that there are many things in the world that are unfair and unjust. They know that there are individuals and nations who use their power and authority to ill-treat others and deny them their proper human rights. Even then they believe that war and violence are always wrong. All disputes, even major international incidents, should be settled by peaceful means.

During wars pacifists who are called to serve in the armed forces state that they are **conscientious objectors**. Some have served with immense courage as stretcher-bearers or medical staff. Although they risk being killed, they will not kill.

Quakers (members of the Society of Friends) are Christians who believe that war is always wrong because they believe

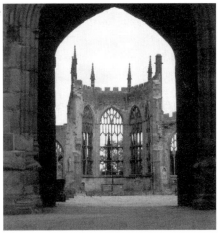

- there is something of God in all people
- more can be gained by appealing to the love and goodness, in ourselves and in others, than by threats
- 'weapons of the spirit' – love, non-violence, kindness, laughter – are weapons that heal and do not destroy. These are the weapons which will defeat evil.

*Cross in Coventry Cathedral*

## Non-violent protest

There are times when complaining against injustice achieves nothing. If reasoned argument does not work, a stronger protest is needed. Many Christians believe that the protest must be non-violent.

A famous example of a non-violent protest is the Montgomery bus boycott in Alabama, USA. This was organized in 1955–6 by Martin Luther King.

- Rosa Parks, a black woman, refused to give up her seat on the bus for a white man. She was arrested for breaking the segregation laws.
- Martin Luther King and other leaders of the black community decided to protest by organizing a boycott of the city bus services.
- Church ministers backed the protest by announcing it at their services.
- 90 per cent of black people who used the buses joined the boycott.
- Even though some black people were harassed and bombs set off at the houses of some of the leaders (including Martin Luther King), the boycott continued without violence.
- After nearly a year the USA Supreme Court ruled that the segregation laws on the buses were illegal. The unjust laws had been defeated by non-violent protest.

## What if pacifism and non-violence do not work?

It is better that evil and injustice are overcome peacefully and without violence. That must always be the ideal.

Sometimes it seems that evil can only be overcome through the use of force.

- Dietrich Bonhoeffer, a German pastor in the 1930's, was a pacifist.
- He joined in non-violent protest against Hitler and Nazism. Hitler was clearly not going to give way to the protest.
- He was torn between his pacifist beliefs and the need to end Hitler's evil regime so very reluctantly he joined a group plotting to assassinate Hitler.

## A just war

The fact that the non-violent approach does not always work does not mean that war is automatically justified. Certain conditions need to be met before Christians consider that a war is 'just'.

- There must be a just cause. The motive must be right.
- It must be the decision of a government, not an individual.
- It must have a good chance of success.
- Only such force as is absolutely necessary should be used.
- Innocent civilians must not be attacked.
- War must be the final resort.

**beware**

Some students write that Christians will take part in a just war as it involves no killing. This is nonsense!

## Terrorism

Terrorists are people who use extreme violence to achieve what they want, even at the cost of innocent lives. Many terrorists call themselves freedom fighters. They believe strongly in the cause for which they are fighting. They may regard themselves as fighting a just war. Others would not agree. Acts of terrorism fail to meet the conditions for a just war. In particular, most acts of terrorism are not the decisions of governments – or at least no government admits to having been involved. Also, innocent civilians often suffer.

## Nuclear war

Nuclear war poses particular problems because of the massive destruction which could result. The nuclear bomb dropped on the city of Hiroshima (Japan) on 6 August 1945 killed 80,000 to 140,000 immediately, with 100,000 people seriously injured. By 1989 it was believed that the USA and the USSR had between them about 50,000 warheads which had a destructive power one million times greater than that of the Hiroshima bomb. This led to a number of arms reduction treaties and a proposed test ban treaty. In 1995, 178 nations pledged to work for total global nuclear disarmament.

Christians believe that a nuclear war could never meet the conditions of a just war. Many of them have campaigned for nuclear disarmament.

*Could an action such as this ever be justified?*

# Disarmament

> They will beat their swords into ploughshares
> and their spears into pruning hooks.
> Nation will not take up sword against nation,
> nor will they train for war anymore. (Micah 4: 3)

That was the dream of the prophet Micah centuries before the time of Jesus.

Disarmament (getting rid of weapons) is a wonderful ideal. Is it practical?

- Unilateral disarmament is disarmament by one nation regardless of the policies of others. The nation would be showing that they were not a threat to anyone.
- Multilateral disarmament is disarmament by all nations at the same time, in line with each other. There would need to be constant checking and supervision to ensure that all sides kept to the policy.
- Nuclear disarmament is the destruction of all nuclear weapons. Nations would rely on conventional (ordinary, non-nuclear) weapons only.

The success of any disarmament policy relies on complete trust. Between some nations that trust exists. People move freely from one country to another and there is no hint or suggestion of conflict between those neighbouring countries. The question is, could that trust ever lead to complete global disarmament?

**did you know?**

At 10pm every night, tens of thousands of people all over the world link up to pray for God's guidance on the leaders of all nations and for the coming of world understanding and peace.

# Relevant Bible passages

**2A**

Matthew 26: 47–53. When soldiers came to take Jesus by force, he did not resist arrest. When a disciple drew his sword to defend him, Jesus stopped him. Does this make Jesus a pacifist?

Mark 11: 15–18. Jesus went into the temple to find traders there. He drove them out, saying that they were turning the temple into 'a den of robbers'. Was Jesus making a violent protest?

Luke 4: 16–21. Jesus said he was filled with the Spirit of the Lord – the spirit of freedom from fear and oppression.

Romans 13: 1–7. Paul writes about the authority of the state. All authority comes from God. Christians have an obligation to obey authority, including the authority of their government. Does this mean that if a government orders Christians to fight in a war they should do so?

**2B**

Exodus 20: 1–17. The Ten Commandments. One of the commandments is: 'You shall not murder.' Some Christians take this to mean that killing in war is always wrong. Others point out that in Hebrew, the language in which the commandments were written, there are different words for 'murder' and 'kill in battle'.

Matthew 5: 1–12. Among the **Beatitudes** is 'Blessed are the peacemakers, for they will be called sons of God'.

Matthew 5: 38–48. Jesus is talking about some of the teachings of the Old Testament and, in his teaching, goes beyond them.

Jesus said: 'You have heard that it was said, "Eye for eye, and tooth for tooth." But I tell you, Do not resist an evil person. If someone strikes you on the right cheek, turn to him the other also.

You have heard that it was said, "Love your neighbour and hate your enemy." But I tell you, Love your enemies and pray for those who persecute you, that you may be sons of your Father in heaven.'

## Try these short questions

### 2A only

**a** Why did Jesus drive the traders out of the temple? (2 marks)

**b** According to Paul, why should Christians accept the authority of the state? (2 marks)

### 2B only

**c** In the Beatitudes, what did Jesus say about peacemakers? (2 marks)

**d** How did Jesus say a Christian should respond when struck on the cheek? (2 marks)

### 2A and 2B

**e** What is meant by **i** 'pacifist' and **ii** 'terrorist'? (4 marks)

**f** What are the conditions which must be met for a war to be considered a just war? (6 marks)

## Exam-type questions

Explain why some Christians might think it is right to fight in a war. (4 marks)　　　　(NEAB, 2000)

### Student's answer

*They are fighting to protect those they love. They are fighting to protect their homes. Their government has declared war on an enemy which was threatening to harm them and they believe their country is doing right. All other options have been tried and this is the only way to stop the enemy.*

## Examiner's comments

The question is about the 'just war' although the actual words are not used. The candidate has made a number of valuable points. War has been declared by a proper authority – their own government. They believe that the cause is a just one, the protection of their homes, their loved ones and themselves. The action is the last resort after everything else has been tried. Not every aspect of the just war is covered, but the candidate may think that some aspects are arguments against fighting. Even so, the candidate could have stated that some Christians might think that civilian casualties are justified if the cause is good enough.

There is no reference here to the teaching of Jesus or of any Christian leader. The candidate might say that when Jesus drove the traders from the temple he used force to get rid of something evil. The candidate might not agree that the incident is relevant here, but it would be a fair point to make.

Mark: 3/4

## Examination practice

**a** Explain why some Christians believe that fighting in a war is always wrong. (4 marks) (NEAB, 2000)

**b** Have the people in this picture the right to make this sort of protest? Give reasons for your answer, showing that you have considered more than one point of view. (5 marks)

## Checklist for revision

| | Understand and know | Need more revision | Do not understand |
|---|---|---|---|
| I know what a pacifist is. | ☐ | ☐ | ☐ |
| I know what is meant by a conscientious objector. | ☐ | ☐ | ☐ |
| I can list six conditions for a just war. | ☐ | ☐ | ☐ |
| I can give an example of a non-violent protest. | ☐ | ☐ | ☐ |
| I can give two examples of relevant incidents in the life of Jesus. | ☐ | ☐ | ☐ |

# 22 Crime, punishment and forgiveness 1D 2A 2B

## Topic summary

- Crime is present in all societies. Laws are set up by the state, or country, to protect society from the criminal acts of others.
- There are five main *aims* of punishment. There are also different *types* of punishment, which range in severity depending on the nature of the crime.
- **Capital punishment** is used in some countries to punish those who have committed the most serious of crimes. Christians are divided as to whether the execution of a person is ever right.
- Jesus never taught that a person should not be punished for something they had done wrong. He taught of the importance of forgiveness from others for those who do wrong.

## What do I need to know?

- The difference between crime and sin. The causes of crime.
- The five main aims of punishment – retribution, deterrence, protection, reformation and vindication.
- The Christian aims of reformation and **reconciliation**.
- Capital punishment and the different responses of Christians to the death penalty.
- Bible passages about the importance of forgiving those who have done wrong.
  - **1D** Matthew 6: 5–15; Luke 5: 17–26; Luke 5: 27–32; Luke 7: 36–50; Luke 15: 1–32
  - **2A** Matthew 5: 38–48; Matthew 18: 23–35; Luke 15: 11–32; Luke 23: 32–43; John 8: 2–11; Romans 13: 1–7
  - **2B** Luke 15: 1–10; Luke 15: 11–32; Matthew 18: 23–35

## Crime and sin

People commit a crime when they break the law. Laws are set up by the state or country to keep peace and order among people. Breaking one of these laws is a criminal offence for which punishments are laid down.

People sin when they go against the law or will of God. A sin can be a wrong action – for example, theft. It can also be a wrong thought – for example, jealousy. Most crimes are also sins, but a number of sins are not seen as crimes. An example is **adultery**.

## What are the causes of crime?

There are a number of circumstances which may lead people to commit a crime.

- Poverty – for some people, turning to crime is the only way they can afford the basic necessities of life.

- Envy – some feel that it is unfair that they have so little compared to others.

- Drugs – some people need to commit crime to find the money to buy more drugs.

- Prejudice – hatred of another group of people because of their race, colour or religion may lead to civil unrest, injury and even murder.

- Peer pressure – young people may feel pressurized into committing crime rather than be ridiculed by their friends.

- Boredom – some young people and unemployed adults commit crime as they feel they have nothing else to do.

- Lack of deterrence – some argue that the rate of crime is increasing because modern methods of punishment are not severe enough to put people off from committing crime.

## The five aims of punishment 2A 2B

A country's justice system does not punish criminals just for the sake of it. There are aims to punishment – or expected outcomes.

1 PROTECTION – society needs to be protected from those who commit crime, particularly from those who are guilty of murder or rape. Imprisonment keeps society safe and also protects offenders against themselves.

2 DETERRENCE – it is hoped that people punished for a crime will not break the law again. Also, others who are considering a crime may be put off by the punishments they see others receiving.

3 RETRIBUTION – someone who commits a crime should receive a punishment that fits the crime. The victim 'gets even' on the criminal, based on the Old Testament idea of 'a life for a life, an eye for an eye and a tooth for a tooth' (Deuteronomy 19: 21). In other words, a murderer is executed and a thief who steals loses his freedom.

4 VINDICATION – if society is to be safe, crime must be punished. Criminals must be shown that crime will not be tolerated and that the law must be respected.

5 REFORM – rather than seeking revenge, this aim of punishment tries to help the criminal see the wrong they have done and **repent**. The person will not go back to their old way of life and will have something positive to offer society when they are released. Reform is sometimes called the Christian aim of punishment. Jesus often spoke of the need to forgive those who have done wrong and help them to reform.

## The Christian aim of reform 1D 2A 2B

Many Christians, and non-Christians, prefer the aim of reform. They follow the example of Jesus, who did not teach against punishment but taught his followers to forgive those who had done wrong to them.

Reform is seen as a positive reaction to crime. If offenders see the error of their ways and are sorry, they are less likely to re-offend. Something positive can come out of a negative situation. Prisons offer the services of chaplains and counsellors to help offenders to reform.

See page 60, on the Sacrament of Reconciliation.

Christian Churches offer their congregations the opportunity to repent of their wrong actions. Jesus taught his followers the importance of repentance, of the need to be genuinely sorry and to ensure that the wrong action or thought is not repeated. The Roman Catholic Church, for example, offers the **Sacrament** of Reconciliation. A person, known as the penitent, asks for God's forgiveness through a priest. The penitent confesses his or her sins to the priest and is given a **penance**, or act to perform to show repentance. The priest gives the penitent **absolution** if true repentance has been shown. Other **traditions** have a point in the service where the **congregation** can confess their sins in silence to God. The priest or minister will say a prayer of absolution for everyone after this.

Christians believe that true repentance brings reconciliation with God – freedom from sin means that the relationship between God and the penitent is restored. For many Christians, this is a great source of relief and comfort.

# Capital punishment 2A 2B

This is the severest type of punishment – it is punishment by death. In some countries, a person who has been found guilty of a terrible crime, such as murder or terrorism, may be executed. Methods of execution include the electric chair, lethal injection, hanging and shooting. In a number of states in the USA, execution follows a period of a few years on 'death row'. In some areas of the world, political prisoners are sometimes executed without trial.

Capital punishment is no longer a method of punishment in the UK.

As with all other people, Christians are divided over the rights and wrongs of capital punishment. Either side can back up their opinions with passages from the Bible.

### 'Yes' to capital punishment

Christians who are in favour of capital punishment may make the following comments.

- Life is sacred, it is a gift from God. Anyone who takes the life of another should pay with their own. Christians who believe this use the Old Testament idea of 'an eye for an eye, a tooth for a tooth' to support their argument.
- Capital punishment protects society. It makes sure that a murderer, for example, cannot possibly re-offend. The death penalty shows society's hatred of murder. Genesis 9: 6 states, 'Whoever sheds the blood of man, by man shall his blood be shed; for in the image of God has God made man.'
- 'Life sentence' does not always mean what it says. Many criminals are released from prison within a few years. Without the death penalty, murder is not treated severely enough.

**did you know?**
Capital punishment has been abolished in 107 countries around the world.

- Capital punishment acts as a deterrent for those who are considering murder.
- It is more merciful to execute a criminal rather than making them stay in prison for many years, often in solitary confinement.
- Capital punishment may help the victim's family to come to terms with their loss. They may feel that a just payment has been made for the life of a loved one.

## 'No' to capital punishment

Christians who are against capital punishment may make the following comments.

- If life is sacred, then so is the criminal's. What right has society to judge when a person's life should end? Jesus changed the Old Testament idea of 'an eye for an eye'. He told his followers that they should not seek revenge; they should forgive and 'turn the other cheek' (Matthew 5: 38–9). He also said that they should pray for those who have done them harm.
- One of the Ten Commandments says, 'You shall not murder.' Execution is murder. How can the law condemn murder and then kill in the name of the law? Does that not make the executioner a murderer too?
- In the past, mistakes have been made. A number of people have been executed and later found to be innocent.
- There is no evidence to prove that capital punishment is a deterrent. Countries that use capital punishment have as many serious crimes as those that do not.
- Capital punishment takes away, or lessens, the opportunity for reform and repentance. A prison sentence makes this possible.
- The death penalty is inhumane. How can those who practise it claim to love their neighbour as themselves?

## Relevant Bible passages

### 2A Matthew 5: 38–48. Teaching on forgiveness

Jesus takes the Old Testament idea of 'an eye for an eye' (Deuteronomy 19) and changes it completely. His followers must not take revenge. He adds, 'If someone strikes you on the right cheek, turn to him the other also.' This is not an easy command to follow; it is human nature to retaliate. Jesus is not saying that crimes should go unpunished, nor that they should be brushed under the carpet and forgotten. He says that revenge and retaliation are not to be the characteristics of his followers. Instead he says, 'Love your enemies and pray for those who persecute you.' There are other solutions to a problem than revenge.

### 2A 2B Matthew 18: 23–35. The unmerciful servant

The king in the **parable** represents God who forgives sin. The parable teaches that if we want God to forgive us then we must be prepared to forgive the sins of others. Although the servant in the story is forgiven, he is not prepared, in turn, to forgive the smaller sin of another. Jesus warns that God will punish those who do not forgive.

### 1D 2A 2B Luke 15: 11–32. The forgiving father/lost son

The forgiving father represents God. All people sin – they are represented by the

**beware**

Jesus never taught that punishment is wrong. To say that he did is a common mistake in exam answers.

**hints and tips**

Christians believe that God forgives sin. However, in return, they must be prepared to forgive those who wrong them.

younger son. Yet God waits for them to see the error of their ways and return to him. When they do, God rejoices and welcomes them back with open arms. The elder son represents those who believe that some sins cannot be forgiven. Jesus teaches that Christians must learn to forgive those who repent, just as God does.

### 2A Luke 23: 32–43. The penitent thief

One of the thieves on the cross understood that Jesus was innocent but believed that he, himself, deserved his punishment. He asked Jesus to remember him in heaven. Jesus forgave the man and said, 'Today you will be with me in paradise.' This incident shows Christians that it is never too late to repent.

### 2A John 8: 2–11. The woman caught committing adultery

Some religious leaders brought to Jesus a woman who had been caught in the act of adultery. Jewish Law said that this was a sin punishable by death. If Jesus had said that the woman should not be stoned, the leaders would have accused him of going against the Law of Moses. If he had said that the woman should be stoned, the leaders would have accused him of going against his teaching of mercy. Jesus said neither of these things. He said that anyone in the crowd who had never sinned could throw the first stone. Of course, all people sin and the crowd slowly left. Jesus makes no comment on the use of capital punishment, nor does he say that the death penalty is wrong. Instead, he says that, as we have all sinned, it is not possible to throw the first stone. We should not judge others when we have sinned ourselves.

The important message of the story comes at the end when Jesus says to the woman, 'Neither do I condemn you. Go now and leave your life of sin.' The woman has been given a chance to repent and sin no more.

### 1D 2B Luke 15: 1–10. The parables of the lost sheep and the lost coin

These two parables are similar to the parable of the lost son. One sheep from a flock and one coin are lost. A great and loving search is made for that which is lost. When it is found there is great rejoicing. In the same way, Jesus teaches that there is great rejoicing in heaven when one sinner repents and returns to the family of God.

### 1D Luke 5: 17–26. Jesus' authority to forgive sins

When Jesus sees the faith of the paralysed man and his friends he says to the paralysed man, 'Friend, your sins are forgiven.' The religious leaders accused Jesus of blasphemy, as they believed that only God could forgive sins. Jesus asked whether it is easier to make a paralysed man walk or forgive him of his sins. Both things are possible for Jesus. To prove his point, he told the man to get up and go home. Jesus has the power to forgive the sins of those who ask and to change their lives around.

### 1D Luke 5: 27–32. Eating with sinners

This passage describes the call of Levi, or Matthew, to be one of Jesus' disciples. Levi was a tax collector, a man despised by his people as tax collectors helped the Romans and demanded too much money in tax. Later, Levi invited Jesus to a banquet at his house along with some of his friends who were considered to be sinners and outcasts by Jewish society. When the Jewish leaders complained about Jesus mixing with such people he said that it is the sick who need a doctor, not those who are well. Jesus said that his mission from God was to 'call sinners to repentance'. Those who repent will be forgiven by God.

### 1D Matthew 6: 5–15. The Lord's Prayer

This is also a useful additional passage for students studying **2A** and **2B**.

The prayer that Jesus taught his followers to say contains a section on the importance of forgiveness: 'Forgive us our debts, as we also have forgiven our debtors.' The words 'debts' and 'debtors' can mean 'sins' and 'those who sin against us'.

See page 89 on the Lord's Prayer. What does it say about forgiveness?

## Try these short questions

**a** What can Christians learn about forgiveness from the parable of the forgiving father/lost son? (4 marks)

**b** Identify a Bible passage you have studied which teaches the importance of repentance and/or reform. What lessons can be learnt from this passage? (4 marks)

## Exam-type questions

**a** 'An eye for eye, tooth for tooth; but I tell you …' What did Jesus add to this saying? (2 marks)

**b** Why do some Christians believe that capital punishment is wrong? (5 marks)     (NEAB, 1996)

### Student's answer

*a Jesus said that a person should not take revenge on someone who harms them. They should 'turn the other cheek'. He also said that we should love our enemies and pray for those who persecute us.*

*b Some Christians believe that capital punishment breaks the Commandment, 'You shall not murder.' The killing of another person is wrong whatever the circumstances and that includes the death penalty. The Bible teaches that life is precious and that only God has the right to take it away.*

*Jesus showed that he did not approve of capital punishment when he stopped the execution of a woman who had committed adultery. Capital punishment goes against the Christian aim of reform.*

## Examiner's comments

**a**   The student has given a full answer for two marks.                                    Mark: 2/2

**b**   The student has given a passage from the Bible which can be used as an argument against capital punishment. The fact that the Bible teaches that life is precious and God-given is also correct. However, the student should not have stated that the story of the woman caught in adultery proves that Jesus was against capital punishment. Jesus did not say that it was wrong. The story shows the importance of not judging others, of forgiveness and reform. The student's last sentence, whilst correct, lacks detail and explanation.

The student could have given more reasons why some Christians are against capital punishment (see page 123) and more examples of Jesus' teaching on forgiveness and repentance. Much more could have been said here.                                    Mark: 2/5

## Examination practice

**a**   What is the difference between crime and sin? (2 marks)

**b**   Name three of the causes of crime. (3 marks)

**c**   Why do Christians believe that reform is the most important aim of punishment? (3 marks)

## Checklist for revision

|  | Understand and know | Need more revision | Do not understand |
|---|:---:|:---:|:---:|
| I understand the causes of crime. | ☐ | ☐ | ☐ |
| I can identify the five aims of punishment. | ☐ | ☐ | ☐ |
| I understand and can explain the importance of the aim of reform for Christians. | ☐ | ☐ | ☐ |
| I can give at least four reasons both for and against capital punishment. I can also include Bible passages to support both arguments. | ☐ | ☐ | ☐ |
| I can identify and explain a number of Jesus' teachings on forgiveness, judgement and repentance. | ☐ | ☐ | ☐ |

# 23 Marriage and divorce

1A 1B 2A 2B

## Topic summary

- Christians look upon marriage as a gift from God. They believe that God created humans male and female so that they would fall in love, marry and have children.
- Christians regard marriage as a life-long commitment and the appropriate relationship in which to have sex and to raise children.
- In a Christian marriage **ceremony**, husband and wife are joined together by God. They promise to put their partner first in all things and to remain faithful for life.
- Sadly, some marriages fail. Christian traditions vary in their attitude towards divorce and remarriage.

## What do I need to know?

- The importance Christians place on the married state.
- A knowledge of what happens at a Christian marriage ceremony and the promises the man and woman make to each other.
- **2A** **2B** The attitudes of different Christian traditions to divorce, **annulment**, remarriage and to sexual relationships outside marriage.
- **2A** **2B** Bible passages on the subject of marriage.

  **2A** Exodus 20: 1–17; Matthew 5: 27–32; 1 Corinthians 6: 18–20; Ephesians 5: 21–33

  **2B** Mark 10: 2–9

## The meaning of Christian marriage

> God created human beings in his own image,
> in the image of God he created them; male and
> female he created them. God blessed them and
> said to them, 'Be fruitful and increase in number.'
> (Genesis 1: 27–8)
> A man will leave his father and mother and be
> united to his wife, and they will become one flesh.
> (Genesis 2: 24)

For Christians, marriage has been from the beginning an important part of God's plan for human beings. Christians believe it is God's intention that

- a man and woman should fall in love and live permanently and faithfully together as husband and wife
- as a result and expression of their love, they have sexual intercourse
- children are born and nurtured in a loving family environment.

A Christian marriage ceremony takes place in the presence of God. Promises made by the couple are made to each other in front of God. Marriage is seen as a total commitment between two people and a relationship in which love is given freely and uniquely for the rest of their lives. This is the Christian ideal of marriage and the ideal environment in which to bring up children.

> Marriage is a gift of God in **creation** through which husband and wife may know the **grace** of God.
>
> It is given that as man and woman grow together in love and trust, they shall be united with one another in heart, body and mind, as Christ is united with his bride, the Church.
>
> The gift of marriage brings husband and wife together in the delight and tenderness of sexual union and joyful commitment to the end of their lives.
>
> It is given as the foundation of family life in which children are [born and] nurtured …
>
> No one should enter into it lightly or selfishly but reverently and responsibly in the sight of almighty God.
>
> *From the Church of England's Book of Common Worship.*

## Marriage as a sacrament

A sacrament is a ceremony through which Christians come to know God's love and mercy more. Roman Catholics, Orthodox Christians and a number of Anglicans look upon marriage as a sacrament. They believe that this sacrament invites God into the relationship between husband and wife – he is present as they exchange their vows and will remain with them throughout their life together, helping them and strengthening their love for each other.

## The marriage ceremony 1A 1B

There are a number of important points in a Christian marriage ceremony which are common to most traditions.

- The priest or minister introduces the ceremony with an explanation of the importance and meaning of Christian marriage.
- The bride and groom make vows of life-long commitment to each other.
- Rings are given and received.
- The groom and bride are officially pronounced man and wife.
- Prayers are said for the couple and they are blessed.
- The marriage register is signed by the couple and witnessed by family and friends. This act makes the marriage legally valid.

### The making of vows

In every Christian marriage ceremony, the bride and groom make vows, or solemn promises, to each other. This is usually thought to be the point at which the couple become married. The following vows are taken from the Roman Catholic marriage rite. Vows taken by Christians from other traditions are similar.

The couple turn and say to each other in turn:

> I call upon these persons here to witness
> that I, *Name*, do take thee, *Name*,
> to be my lawful wedded wife/husband
> to have and to hold from this day forward,
> for better, for worse,
> for richer, for poorer,
> in sickness and in health,
> to love and to cherish,
> till death do us part.

The Church of England Book of Common Worship adds these words:

> According to God's holy law, and in the presence of God I make this vow.

These vows represent a serious commitment to each other. Before the marriage ceremony, the priest would have explained the meaning of the vows carefully to the couple. They promise in front of God, their family and friends to stay together and stand by each other whatever happens.

- Through good and bad times they will support each other.
- When money is tight they will manage together.
- When serious illness strikes one of the partners, the other is committed to caring for him or her.
- They will love, respect and look after each other, always putting their partner first.
- Only the death of one of them ends the marriage. The commitment is lifelong.

## Exchange of rings

After the vows have been made, the couple will exchange rings. The ring symbolizes two things:

- as a ring is a circle with no beginning or end, it is a sign of their never ending love and faithfulness (fidelity) to each other;
- it is a visible sign of the promises they have made to each other.

# A Roman Catholic marriage ceremony

A Roman Catholic marriage ceremony usually takes place during a **Nuptial Mass**, particularly if both partners are Catholic.

- The bridegroom, his best man and the guests arrive first. Shortly afterwards, the bride arrives with her attendants and is escorted into church by her father or a male representative of the family.
- The priest welcomes everybody and then prays for the bride and groom – 'With faith in you and in each other they pledge their love today. May their lives bear witness to the reality of that love.'
- During the Liturgy of the Word, the readings from the Bible and the priest's homily, or sermon, are concerned with the meaning of Christian marriage.

- The couple and their guests are reminded that marriage is a sacrament, a gift of God's grace to help them keep their vows throughout their married life.

- The bridegroom and bride are questioned by the priest. The three questions asked emphasize the important points of Christian marriage.

  1  'Are you ready freely and without reservation to give yourselves to each other in marriage?' – Christian marriage is an exclusive partnership. Husband and wife remain faithful to each other, just as God is faithful.

  2  'Are you ready to love and honour each other as man and wife for the rest of your lives?' – Christian marriage is permanent; it has no end, as God's love has no end.

  3  'Are you ready to accept children lovingly from God, and bring them up according to the Law of Christ and his church?' – the love of Christian marriage is life-giving, as God loves the world he created. The couple promise to provide a loving and secure Christian home for their children.

- The couple make their vows to each other in front of God and their guests. They exchange rings as a sign of their love and fidelity.

- The couple are pronounced man and wife. They are blessed and the words of Jesus are repeated – 'What God has joined together let no man put asunder.'

- The Nuptial Mass continues; husband and wife receive Holy Communion with their friends and family. Taking Holy Communion at a marriage ceremony, when the bridegroom and bride publicly proclaim their love and commitment to each other, is a **symbol** of the love of Christ represented by the bread and wine.

- Prayers are offered for the couple at the start of their married life together. This is followed by a Nuptial Blessing. The bridegroom, bride, priest and a minimum of two witnesses sign the marriage register. The couple are now married in the eyes of God, the Church and the State.

## When marriages break down  2A  2B

The marriage ceremony marks the beginning of the adventure of wedded life. Couples usually begin this adventure deeply in love and with the intention of keeping the vows they have made to each other. But sometimes things can go wrong.

All husbands and wives experience difficulties during their married lives. Sometimes, the problems can become overwhelming, leading to a loss of love and a breakdown in the marital relationship. There are counselling groups available to couples who feel they need help to resolve their marital difficulties.

> **did you know?**
> Over 40 per cent of marriages in the United Kingdom fail. Why do you think Christians continue to marry?

- Relate – this is a non-Christian organization, but many Christian families use their services or are advisors. Relate counsellors offer relationship education, sex therapy and support for the couple and their families.

- Marriage Care – this is a Roman Catholic organization. It specializes in working with couples who are experiencing marital problems. Counsellors help them to resolve their difficulties. They also help young people prepare for marriage.

What if a couple's problems cannot be resolved? Christian traditions differ in their opinion of divorce.

# What do the churches say about divorce and remarriage? 2A 2B

The Roman Catholic Church does not accept divorce. Marriage vows are made for life in front of God, the couple are 'one flesh', a union that can only end in death. Those who obtain a divorce from the state are still considered to be married in the eyes of God. They cannot remarry in the Roman Catholic Church while their ex-husband or ex-wife is still alive.

However, the Roman Catholic Church will grant an annulment to those who can prove that something prevented a real marriage from taking place. Reasons for this include:

- the marriage has not been consummated (one partner has refused or is unable to have sex)
- one or both partners were forced into marriage
- one partner either lied about his or her ability to have children or never intended to have children
- one partner concealed, for example, his or her addiction to alcohol or drugs
- one or both partners are discovered to be underage or already married.

Each case is considered carefully by a marriage tribunal and it is often a lengthy business. Those whose marriages are annulled are free to marry someone else in church. However, as annulment is not recognized by the state, a civil divorce is necessary as well.

Although the Church of England is against divorce and believes that married people should try to follow the teachings of Jesus concerning marriage, it understands that sometimes the vows cannot be kept for life. Priests may marry divorced people in church if they feel that the circumstances of the divorce warrant it. Permission must be given by the bishop.

Some Free Churches say that Jesus' teaching on marriage is the ideal – couples should try to live up to it. However, problems can be insurmountable and some Christian marriages do fail. It is thought better to end an unhappy, loveless marriage for all concerned. Free Churches usually accept a civil divorce and allow remarriage.

# Sexual relationships outside marriage 2A 2B

Sex before marriage is known as pre-marital sex or fornication. There has been much debate over the rights and wrongs of sex before marriage. Most Christian traditions teach that sex should be kept for marriage, where a husband and wife show their deep love and commitment to each other by making love. Many Christians believe that by 'saving themselves' for their life partner, the act of love making is more special. Also, sexual intercourse can lead to the creation of new life. Most Christians believe that the marital home is the best place to raise children.

Sex whilst married, with a person who is not your wife or husband, is known as **adultery** (having an affair) or infidelity (unfaithfulness). Christian Churches agree that adultery is wrong and destructive for the following reasons.

- It breaks the vows the couple made to each other at their marriage ceremony – they promised to be faithful until death.
- It breaks the commandment 'You shall not commit adultery' (see page 150) and is against the teaching of Jesus.
- It breaks the bond of trust between husband and wife – trust is an essential factor in a marriage.
- It may destroy the marriage and break up the family home.

## Relevant Bible passages  2A   2B

### 2A  *Matthew 5: 27–32. Adultery and divorce*

The Old Testament law allowed divorce. When questioned on this subject, Jesus shows that he is against divorce, except in cases of adultery. He continues by saying that those who think lustful thoughts about another person have committed adultery in their minds – thoughts can be as bad as actions.

Jesus also says that, in the eyes of God, marriage is for life. Anyone who divorces and marries again commits adultery.

### 2A  *1 Corinthians 6: 18–20. The body as a temple*

Paul speaks of caring for our bodies – they are special, a part of God's creation. The Holy Spirit, a part of God, lives within the bodies of human beings. We should treat our bodies with respect and behave with dignity. Our bodies should not be abused or misused. In the context of this section, these words could refer to sexual intercourse outside of marriage.

### 2A  *Ephesians 5: 21–33. Husbands and wives*

Like Jesus, Paul goes back to the story of creation when he speaks about marriage. A man and woman become one being when they marry. He says that every Christian is part of Christ's body, the Church, and that marital love is a sign of the love which exists between Jesus and the Church – a pure, unselfish and sacrificial love. Wives should respect their husbands and husbands should love their wives as much as themselves.

### 2B  *Mark 10: 2–9. Marriage and divorce*

This is Mark's version of the teaching of Jesus on the subject of marriage and divorce. Jesus refers back to God's intention for men and women at creation. They leave their families and set up their own family unit, they become 'one flesh'. They have been joined together by God and no one else must come between them. In this passage, divorce is not acceptable under any circumstances. The same teaching against marriage following a divorce is given here as in the passage from Matthew above.

## Examiner's comments

**a** This is a sound and well presented answer for two marks. The student could obviously have chosen any one of the vows, but would have to have given an equally full answer. Mark: 2/2

**b** It is true that a couple promise to accept children lovingly from God at their marriage ceremony. However, the student has made having children sound like a mere duty. The student should have added that children are a visible sign of the couple's love; their love gives life, just as God creates life. Mark: ½/2

**c** This is a good answer. Both sides of the argument have been fairly and sensibly treated and the student has come down on one side of the argument, as required. Mark: 5/5

## Examination practice

**a** Why is a ring used as a symbol of Christian marriage? (2 marks)

**b** What is the difference between divorce and annulment? (4 marks)

## Checklist for revision

| | Understand and know | Need more revision | Do not understand |
| --- | --- | --- | --- |
| I understand the importance of marriage for Christians. | ☐ | ☐ | ☐ |
| I know and understand the vows a couple make to each other at their wedding ceremony. | ☐ | ☐ | ☐ |
| I can describe a Christian marriage ceremony. | ☐ | ☐ | ☐ |
| I know what different Christian traditions teach about divorce and remarriage. | ☐ | ☐ | ☐ |
| I understand the difference between divorce and annulment. | ☐ | ☐ | ☐ |

## Topic summary

- **Prejudice** takes many forms and can often lead to **discrimination** based on race, religion, gender, age and disability, amongst others.
- Jesus showed that he was against the prejudices and discrimination of his time by his words and actions.
- A number of well-known Christians have fought against prejudice and discrimination, usually with non-violent action.
- Various passages in the Bible stress the equality of all human beings and the correct attitude Christians should have towards their 'neighbours'.

## What do I need to know?

- The definitions of the terms 'prejudice' and 'discrimination' and the difference between the two. The main types of prejudice and discriminatory behaviour.
- Jesus' stand against the prejudices of his time.
- Examples of discriminatory behaviour, for example, apartheid, the Holocaust.
- Passages from the Bible relevant to this topic.
  - **2A** Luke 7: 1–10; Luke 10: 25–37; Acts 11: 1–18; Galatians 3: 28
  - **2B** Luke 10: 25–37; James 2: 1–9; Luke 7: 1–10
- **2A** The work of a well-known Christian whose beliefs led him or her to campaign against prejudice and discrimination.

## What are prejudice and discrimination?

Prejudice is an unfair thought or action about a person or group because of their race, religion, gender, age, appearance or disability. It is usually based on a lack of understanding and knowledge. An example of prejudice is: 'Women are homemakers. They should stay at home and look after the children.'

Discrimination is prejudice in action. It is when a person or group is treated differently as a result of prejudice. An example of discrimination is: 'This woman should not be offered the job as she ought to be at home with her children.'

Here are a few examples of prejudice.

- *Racism* is prejudice against those of another race or ethnic group. Racists often divide human beings into racial groups; they believe that some of these groups are inferior to their own. A form of racism is colour prejudice. This is prejudice against people of a different colour to one's own. Racial discrimination puts racial prejudice into action. People from a different race or ethnic group are treated unfairly or badly. It can also result in civil unrest.

- Religious prejudice is prejudice against those of another religion, or another **tradition** within the same religion. At its worst, religious prejudice can lead to riots and even war. This can be seen in the unrest between Jews and Muslims in the Holy Land and between Catholics and Protestants in Northern Ireland.

- Gender, or sexual prejudice leads to people being treated differently because they are either male or female. It is based on the attitude that one sex is better in some way than the other. Historically, gender prejudice and discrimination arose from the different roles men and women played in society. Men were dominant in society, the breadwinners and the head of the family. Women were the homemakers and child rearers. Great advances have been made in ensuring that the genders are treated more equally. However, many still feel discriminated against in society and at work because of their gender. They believe that some still have sexist attitudes.

- People are often treated differently if they have a disability. Those in wheelchairs, for example, sometimes find access to buildings and facilities difficult. They find that more able people tend to avoid eye contact with a disabled person and many disabled people feel cut off from the rest of society.

## Why are people prejudiced?

There are a number of reasons why people are prejudiced.

- People inherit many of their prejudices from their parents and wider family circle. We are not born prejudiced – we learn it.
- Others tend to pick up and copy the prejudices of their peers and friends.
- We are sometimes afraid of people or things we do not understand or which are different from us in some way. This leads to discriminatory behaviour.

# The effects of prejudice and discrimination

The effects can range from individuals feeling isolated or bullied to great injustices and even death for a whole race of people.

In the 1930s and 1940s, the Nazis were determined to destroy the Jewish race. It began with gradually taking away their basic human rights and ended in the murder of nearly 6 million Jews in concentration camps. This terrible crime against humanity is known as the Holocaust.

Until the 1990s, there was a system in South Africa called apartheid. This is an Afrikaans word meaning 'separateness' or 'apartness'. It was set up and supported by the white government of South Africa and is one of the most extreme cases of legalized racism in history. Under this system, white and black people were totally separated from each other. Black people were not allowed to vote or to have well paid jobs. They were given poor housing with no running water and their children were taught in separate schools from white children.

**did you know?** The Nazis also persecuted gypsies, homosexuals, the handicapped, Catholics and communists.

# Jesus' lack of prejudice and discrimination

Jesus said, 'Love your neighbour as yourself.' He is the perfect role model for Christians of the way in which all human beings should be treated. Many of the prejudices which affect our modern society were also present in Jesus' day.

**read more**
The Centurions Servant
Luke 7: 1–10.
See page 43.

- *Race.* The Roman Empire had conquered Israel. Many Jews hated the Roman soldiers who took over the land of Israel and forced Roman laws on the people. Yet when a Roman centurion asked Jesus to heal his favourite servant, Jesus did not hesitate. Jesus also praised the faith of the centurion – a man of a different race of people.

- *Religion.* The Jews and the Samaritans hated each other. Jews looked upon the Samaritans as having polluted the Jewish religion as they had married **Gentiles**. When he was asked, 'Who is my neighbour?' by an expert in the Jewish Law, Jesus told him the **parable** of the Good Samaritan (Luke 10: 25–37). The hero of this parable is a Samaritan, not a Jew. In fact, the Jewish characters in the story are not cast in a very good light. The parable makes a good point – everyone is our neighbour, even those of a different faith and culture.

- *Gender.* In Jesus' time a woman's social position was beneath a man's and they were not usually allowed to talk with men on such an important topic as religion. Jesus, on the other hand, showed his appreciation and respect for women and he healed both men and women. Two of his closest friends were Martha and Mary, sisters of Lazarus. Jesus let them listen to him teach as well as serve him food. Women stayed with Jesus during the crucifixion when his male followers ran away. On Easter Day, Jesus appeared first to women and gave them the privilege of spreading the news of the **resurrection**.

- *Disability and appearance.* Jesus felt compassion for all those who suffered from disability or disease. He was not put off by them, nor did he judge them by their appearance. He touched lepers, which would have made him 'unclean' according to Jewish Law; he held the hands of the blind and the deaf and of the dead daughter of Jairus before he raised her.

# Christian campaigners against prejudice and discrimination

There have been many Christians who have worked hard against prejudice, discrimination and injustice wherever they have found them. They have been **inspired** and influenced by the teachings and actions of Jesus.

**hints and tips**

Students studying specifications **1D** and **2B** may wish to refer to one of these Christians in the exam.

## Archbishop Desmond Tutu

- Desmond Tutu, born near Johannesburg in South Africa in 1931, grew up with first-hand experience of the injustices of apartheid. It led him to decide to help others in the same situation by becoming a priest.
- Tutu preached against apartheid from the earliest days of his priesthood. He toured South Africa giving lectures, which included examples from the Bible showing God's disapproval of injustice and cruel leadership.
- Tutu chose non-violent protest. He led marches and boycotts and collected petitions.
- His rise to the position of Bishop of Lesotho in 1976 gave Tutu the chance to campaign with more authority. He often told the South African government that its racist approach went against the will of God. Apartheid defied the teachings of Jesus, on which Tutu based his life.
- In 1985, Tutu was awarded the Nobel Peace Prize for his non-violent work to bring an end to apartheid. A while later, he publicly stated that apartheid was 'one of the most vicious systems since Nazism'.
- Tutu became the first black Anglican Archbishop of Cape Town in 1986. He has used his position not only to campaign in South Africa, but has travelled to other countries to persuade governments to join the struggle against inequality and injustice. This work has continued even though apartheid has officially ended.
- Throughout his life, reading the Bible and prayer have always been important to him. Tutu's vision is of a South Africa where black and white people will live together in peace and where 'all people will matter because they are human beings made in the image of God'.

**hints and tips**

You will not be expected to give a biography of the Christian you choose – just details of their work. Always ensure that you refer to a Christian teaching or a passage from the Bible when explaining what influenced them to do the work they did.

## Martin Luther King

Martin Luther King, an ordained minister of the Baptist Church, spent the majority of his adult life campaigning against the segregation of black people in the USA. In one of his many speeches, he said, 'I have a dream that my four little children will one day live in a nation where they will not be judged by the colour of their skin but by the content of their character.' See page 115 for more information about Martin Luther King.

> I have a dream that one day all God's children, blacks, whites, Jews, Gentiles, Protestants and Catholics will be able to join hands and sing in the words of the black people's old song, 'free at last, free at last, thank God Almighty, we are free at last.'
>
> (Martin Luther King, March 1963)

## Relevant Bible passages

**2A** **2B** *Luke 10: 25–37. The Good Samaritan*

Jesus told this parable having been asked by an expert in Jewish Law, 'Who is my neighbour?' Those listening to Jesus' story would have expected the Jewish priest and the Levite to help the victim, who was a Jew. However, the hero of the story is not a Jew, but a Samaritan – Jews and Samaritans hated each other. The Samaritan not only tends to the victim's wounds, but also pays an innkeeper to look after him until he is well. Jesus ends the parable by saying, 'Go and do likewise.'

## 2A  *Acts 11: 1–18. Peter and Cornelius*

As a Jew, Peter would have believed that only certain foods were kosher, or fit to eat. In his dream, he saw all types of food, kosher and non-kosher, mixed up together. Peter was horrified when he was told by God to eat the food – an order that had to be given three times. God told Peter that he had created everything clean. Peter explained later that he probably would not have gone to Cornelius' house if he had not had the dream. Cornelius was a Gentile and Peter would have believed that entering the house would have made him unclean. God had shown that the **Gospel** was for Gentiles too. There is no difference between 'clean' people (the Jews) and 'unclean' people (the Gentiles) – they are all invited into God's kingdom and equally loved by him.

## 2A  *Galatians 3: 28. All one in Christ*

In his letter to the Galatians, Paul explains that all people are equal to God. God does not love one group more than another, 'for you are all one in Christ Jesus.'

## 2B  *James 2: 1–9. Respect for all people*

This is a good passage to show how our prejudices can lead to discrimination. Many would give more time and priority to a rich person than to one who is poor and shabbily dressed. This is discrimination based on the prejudice that the poor are somehow less important than the rich. This type of behaviour is hated by God, who loves all people equally. To treat someone differently because of their appearance or the amount of money they possess is wrong.

### Try these short questions

**a**  Explain the difference between 'prejudice' and 'discrimination'. (2 marks)
(NEAB, 1999)

**b**  What can Christians learn about Jesus' attitude to people of different races and religions from the parable of the Good Samaritan? (2 marks)   (NEAB, 2001)

### Exam-type questions

Why do Christians believe that prejudice is wrong? (3 marks)                    (NEAB, 1999)

#### Student's answer

*Christians believe that prejudice is against the will of God. It is pre-judging a person or a group of people without really knowing them or understanding them. Prejudice leads to discrimination, when people are treated badly or unfairly because of their colour, race, religion or disability. Jesus was not prejudiced – he knew that everyone is loved equally by God. He helped and cared for people even if they were of a different colour, race or religion to him; like the centurion's servant. He also told the story of the Good Samaritan which shows that everyone in the world is our neighbour and should be treated as we would like to be treated. Christians try to follow Jesus' example.*

## Examiner's comments

The student has done well to explain the meaning of 'prejudice', particularly if this has not been asked for in a previous question. The answer clearly states that prejudice is against the will of God and continues by giving examples from the Bible of times when Jesus helped those who were usually discriminated against at the time. A good and full answer for three marks.          Mark: 3/3

## Examination practice

**a**  Explain why some Christians do not agree with gender discrimination. (3 marks)

**b**  'Everyone should be treated equally.' Do you agree? Give reasons for your answer, showing that you have thought about more than one point of view. You must refer to Christianity in your answer. (6 marks)                                                                       (AQA, 2002)

# Checklist for revision

| | Understand and know | Understand and know | Understand and know |
|---|---|---|---|
| I understand the difference between 'prejudice' and 'discrimination'. | ☐ | ☐ | ☐ |
| I can list four of the major types of prejudice. | ☐ | ☐ | ☐ |
| I can give reasons why prejudice begins. | | | |
| I can give examples of times when Jesus went against the prejudices of his day. | ☐ | ☐ | ☐ |
| I can describe the work of one Christian who worked against prejudice and discrimination. | ☐ | ☐ | ☐ |
| I can explain at least three passages from the Bible relevant to this topic. | ☐ | ☐ | ☐ |

# 25 Aid to developing countries

## Topic summary

- The world can be divided into two areas – the North and the South. Everyday items, which people in the North consider to be basic to their needs, are looked upon as luxuries by those in the South.

- Food, clean water, health care, education and paid work are basic needs. Many individuals in the world do not have these things.

- The problems of people who live in **developing countries** are made worse by the fact that their governments are heavily in debt to richer countries.

- There are over 6 billion humans in the world. This raises questions concerning over-population and whether the earth's resources are fairly distributed.

- A number of Christian international organizations work to relieve the suffering and bring hope to the world's poorest people. Their work includes short and **long term aid**.

- Christians follow the example of Jesus who gave a special place to the poor in his life and teaching.

## What do I need to know?

- The difference in lifestyle between the world's rich and poor.
- Issues relating to disease, population and debt.
- About short and long term aid.
- The work of one of the following agencies: Christian Aid, CAFOD, Trócaire or Tearfund.
- Bible passages on the subject of caring for others less fortunate than ourselves.
  - **2A** **2B**  Matthew 25: 31–46
  - **2A**  Luke 12: 13–21; Luke 16: 19–31; Acts 4: 32–37

## Rich world, poor world

Our televisions often bring harrowing scenes of human disaster and despair into our living rooms. These are caused, among other things, by natural disasters, poverty, disease, national debt and unfair trading. These scenes raise questions: What are the causes of extreme poverty? Why are some parts of the world wealthier than others? What can be done to help?

It was once common to talk of the poorer countries as being 'Third World Nations' and materially rich countries as 'First World Nations'. Nowadays, many people consider these terms to be inappropriate as they seem to suggest that 'First World' is more important than 'Third World'. Instead, many would consider it more correct to use the terms North and South and to refer to poorer nations as 'developing countries'.

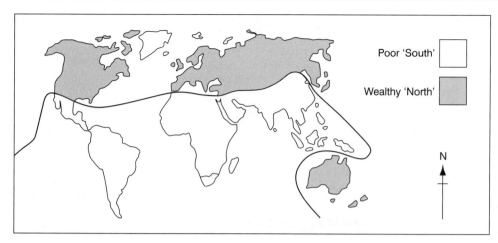

Poor 'South' □

Wealthy 'North' ▨

N ↑

*The map shows the world divided into materially rich and poor countries. The rich countries are sometimes referred to as the North and the poorer countries as the South. The map shows that, with few exceptions, there is a definite North/South divide.*

Look at these facts.

- 20 per cent of the world's human population live in the North and they use 80 per cent of the world's resources; 80 per cent live in the poorer South, but they have access to only 20 per cent of the resources.
- Less than half the children living in the South have access to a formal education. Those that do often have to finish their education at the end of primary school.
- On any given day, over a quarter of the people living in the South will be hungry – many of them will be starving. Yet experts have said that there is more than enough food in the world if it were distributed fairly.
- On average, people in the North can expect to live to at least 70 years of age; many enjoy much longer lives than this. In the South, the average life expectancy is 50 years. **Malnutrition**, extreme poverty and poor health care are partially responsible for this.

## What are the causes of poverty?

1 *Debt.* Large amounts of money were lent to countries in the developing world when interest rates were low. This money was meant to fund health care, schools and industry, but was often misused by their own corrupt governments. When interest rates rose, many developing countries were left owing vast sums to the World Bank and the International Monetary Fund (IMF). Money which could be spent on the basic needs of people in the South is being used to pay interest on debts.

2 *Lack of education.* Most people in the North have access to free education – it is thought to be their right. However, over a third of people in the South are illiterate. One of the main reasons for this is that, in many poorer countries, education is not free and families cannot afford to educate their children. A good education raises a person's standard of living anywhere in the world.

- It helps them to find a good job – one that will raise enough money to support a family comfortably.
- It teaches people their rights and helps them to express their needs.
- It provides important information about health care and hygiene. A large

## Try these short questions

**a** Give one reason why marriage is important to Christians. (3 marks)

**b** Briefly outline one Bible passage that Christians might use to support their belief that divorce is wrong. (2 marks)

## Exam-type questions

**a** Choose one of the marriage vows. Why is it considered an important part of marriage? (2 marks)
(AQA, 2002)

**b** Explain what the Roman Catholic Church means when it teaches that marriage is 'life giving'. (2 marks)
(NEAB, 2000)

**c** 'A Christian couple should be allowed to live together before they get married.' Do you agree? Give reasons for your answer, showing that you have thought about more than one point of view. (5 marks)

### Student's answer

*a* One of the marriage vows is 'in sickness and in health'. An illness or accident may leave one partner helpless. With this vow, the other is committed to caring for him or her. Marital love should not be given just in times of health; it is even more important when one of the partners is vulnerable and in need of care.

*b* Roman Catholics believe that one of the duties of a married couple is to have children. Marriage is the right environment in which to bring up children.

*c* I do not agree with this statement. Those who live together usually have sex. The Bible says that sex is for marriage only; for Christians, it is a gift from God for those who have committed themselves to each other for life. Without the commitment of marriage it is far easier to move on to another partner. What if a child is conceived? Some couples may then get married for the wrong reasons. If two people really love each other enough to live together, why not get married? Is a trial run really necessary? Marriage is a union of two people who really want to spend the rest of their lives together. Unlike a new car, it does not need a test run!

Other people may disagree. They may argue that, with 40 per cent of marriages failing, it is better to find out if you are compatible with your partner before committing yourself to a marriage that might not last. Divorce can be a very painful experience. Today's society accepts couples living together and there is no commandment in the Bible that says this should not be done.

number of people in poorer countries die at an early age from cholera and dysentery – education could prevent this. Sex education raises awareness of the importance of 'safe sex' and how this can be used to prevent the spread of HIV/AIDS. This is particularly important in the South, where HIV/AIDS has devastated whole communities.

- It teaches skills that can be used to raise productivity at work. This is important for those who are self-employed and where families depend on the success of a small farm or industry for their survival.

3  *The rise in population.* Today, there are over 6 billion people in the world and the figure is rising all the time. Although most couples are having less children in the North, due to modern methods of contraception, more children are surviving to adulthood. Resources are being stretched as more people need them.

In poorer countries, many couples have large families because they *are* poor. A farmer in the South, for example, needs labourers to help him with his work. These labourers expect to be paid more than he can afford and so he has children who will help him in the fields. As so many children die at a young age in the South, he will have a number of children to protect the family's future. The problem is, the more children he has the more expensive it is to feed and clothe them. It is a vicious circle.

It is a fact that contraception is not as readily available to couples in the South. However, having less children would not solve their poverty.

4  *Unfair trading.* Many families in developing countries do not get a fair price in the world market for their skill and the food they produce. This is mainly because international trade is controlled by richer countries. The majority of coffee and cocoa is grown by independent small farmers in the South. Often they are not given a fair price for their produce. Many workers in the South work on large plantations that produce, for example, tea. In many cases, these workers are not given a fair wage for their labour and do not have decent working conditions.

**did you know?**

- Around 35,000 people in the world die from hunger every day.
- Many people in developing countries do not have access to clean water, free schooling, free medical care and social security for unemployed and retired people.
- More money is spent on weapons every day than the world's poorest people live on in a year.

## The poverty cycle

For many people there is no way out of the deprived lifestyles they lead. They are caught in the poverty cycle. It has been said that there are five basic requirements for life – food, water, education, health and work. Without these, human life cannot grow and develop. If you do not have enough food you become weak and cannot work. If your community is poor it cannot afford to supply clean water and this leads to disease. If your family is very poor they cannot afford to educate you if you live in a country where education has to be paid for. Without help, each generation becomes trapped in the poverty cycle.

## Short term and long term aid

There are a number of international agencies, some of which are based in the UK, which give help to communities around the world in cases of disaster and extreme poverty. The aid they give is either short term or long term.

**Short term aid.** This type of aid, also known as 'emergency aid', is given to areas affected by natural disasters or war when those affected need help as quickly as possible. Examples of short term aid are given below.

- Food parcels are airlifted and dropped into devastated areas made difficult to reach by flooding, war or difficult terrain.
- Experts in heat-seeking equipment are sent to find survivors following a serious earthquake.
- Tents, blankets and clothes are sent to provide protection for those who have lost their homes in a natural disaster or who are refugees of war.
- International helpers bury those who have died to prevent the spread of disease.
- Doctors and nurses are sent to give aid to survivors and to vaccinate against diseases.
- Clean water and water purification aids are sent to areas where water supplies have been affected by disaster or conflict.

The aim of short term aid is to give immediate help in a disaster situation. Help needs to be quick and basic in these situations. Long term aid may follow.

**Long term aid.** This type of aid is intended to help people become self-reliant. A number of voluntary agencies, like Christian Aid, support schemes set up by local groups and churches.

Examples of long term aid are set out below.

- In some areas of the developing world, people have to travel over 300 miles if they wish to see a doctor. Individuals can be trained in medicine and health care. This provides doctors, nurses and midwives for a community. Agencies run vaccination and vitamin programmes and teach mothers about hygiene.
- Farmers can be given tools, taught how to use them and be educated in modern farming methods. New crops can be introduced and information given as to how to increase crop yields.
- Funding from international agencies can provide the money to build free schools for local communities and to train individuals as teachers. Many people in the North sponsor the education of individual children in the South.
- Communities can be helped to build wells, which provide clean and safe water for their population.
- Agencies such as Traidcraft and Fair Trade ensure that farmers are given a fair price for the goods they produce and that people have the right to good working conditions. Supermarkets in the UK sell fair trade products such as tea, coffee, chocolate and glassware. Those who buy these products know that a fair price has been given to the workers.

Long term aid helps people to escape the poverty cycle.

## The work of international organizations

There are a number of international Christian agencies that offer short and long term aid to individuals and communities around the world.

> **hints and tips**
>
> Draw attention to the statement of Kuan Tzu: 'Give a man a fish and he has food for a day. Teach him how to fish and he has food for a lifetime.' This is the difference between short and long term aid.

> **did you know?**
>
> 'Send-a-cow' is a scheme for giving a cow to a developing world community and training those who will care for it.

# Christian Aid 2A

**Christian Aid**
We believe in life before death

Christian Aid works with the world's poorest people. It began in the UK at the end of World War II to help with the crisis of homelessness across Europe. Today, the agency works in over 60 countries helping people, regardless of religion or race, to escape the poverty cycle and injustice. They offer short and long term aid. Short term aid is sent wherever it is necessary, for example, in the aftermath of volcanoes, floods and war. In the case of long term aid, Christian Aid supports self-help groups within the communities. These are called Christian Aid Partners.

Christian Aid helps people to help themselves. It provides funding and training so that communities can solve their own problems. It gives them the power to provide an adequate standard of living for themselves and their families. Christian Aid says, 'We believe in life before death.'

## *An example of the work of Christian Aid*

Cambodia in south-east Asia is still suffering from the after-effects of a civil war, which killed over 2 million people. Millions of landmines remain scattered around the country. They continue to kill and maim the population and cause problems with food production and transport to schools and work. Many teachers and doctors were killed in the war.

Christian Aid is working with community partners in Cambodia to overcome the effects of the civil war.

- It supports its partner organization, Health Unlimited, in providing health services for people in the remote areas of Cambodia.
- It works with communities to recover and destroy landmines laid during the civil war and give aid to those injured by the landmines.

**hints and tips**
Your specification asks you to study the work of **one** Christian agency. Make sure you choose an agency suggested by your specification.

read more

You may have studied another agency with your teacher. Find up-to-date information on the work of this agency by visiting its website.

- As a result of the war, many households are now led by women. Christian Aid Partners work to improve women's education and health care and give training in agriculture and animal care.

Christian Aid puts Christian belief into action: working for a fairer world with the poor and those in need.

## CAFOD  2A   2B

CAFOD aims to work 'in partnership to tackle the causes of poverty regardless of race, religion or politics.' Like Christian Aid, CAFOD works in partnership with over 1000 programmes around the world, offering both short term and long term aid. Its long term projects include health care, education and skills training, agricultural development and safe water. CAFOD also campaigns on behalf of the world's poor.

> **did you know?**
>
> The letters CAFOD stand for Catholic Fund for Overseas Development. The agency is run by the Catholic Church in England and Wales.

### An example of the work of CAFOD

CAFOD is supporting a project to bring fresh water to Sartogan, a village in Afghanistan. Over four years of drought have devastated the region; crops have failed and there is little fresh water. Many people have left the village hoping to find a better life and have joined the millions living in refugee camps. CAFOD is working with a local organisation called HAFO to bring clean water to the people of Sartogan. The project is already a great success:

- Old water wells have been deepened and the ancient Afghan network of underground water channels has been repaired.
- Water has been cleansed for the population and an irrigation system now waters the villagers' fields. Crops are growing again.
- The project has provided much needed employment to many villagers who receive payment for their work. The standard of living is improving.
- One villager said in 2002, 'Our village was dying, but now we have water we are born again.'

## Relevant Bible passages

You will be expected to be able to refer to the teachings of Jesus and the early Church in your answers on world poverty and aid to developing countries.

### 2A   2B   Matthew 25: 31–46. The parable of the sheep and the goats

In the **parable**, the sheep are the righteous people, those who go out of their way to help others in need. They follow the teachings of Jesus. The goats represent those who ignore the sufferings of others. Notice the six areas of need and what the righteous people do to help: the hungry are fed, the thirsty are given water, the stranger (perhaps a refugee?) is welcomed, those without clothing are clothed, the sick are cared for and those in prison are visited. These areas of need are no different today, 2000 years on. The organizations mentioned in this chapter work in all these areas around the world. Many Christians believe that it is their duty and their pleasure to help others. In doing this, they are following the example of Jesus.

> **read more**
>
> Other relevant passages are:
> Mark 12: 28–34 (page 36)
> Mark 12: 41–4 (page 50)
> Luke 10: 25–37 (page 138)

Jesus says something very important in this passage: those who help people in need are actually helping Jesus himself.

### 2A  *Luke 12: 13–21. The rich fool*

The man in the parable had more than he needed to live a comfortable life. But rather than sharing the surplus around his more needy neighbours, he planned to store his grain in large barns for the future and then to sit back and enjoy life.

The parable teaches that in death everyone is equal. You cannot take your wealth with you when you die. The man's surplus wealth would have been better spent helping those in need.

In his teaching, Jesus never said that it is wrong to be rich. What matters is our attitude to money and what we do with it.

### 2A  *Luke 16: 19–31. The rich man and Lazarus*

The rich man ignored the suffering of the poor man at his own gate. He could not say that he was not aware of the problem. Whilst Lazarus was rewarded in heaven, the rich man was punished in hell.

Like the rich man, we cannot say that we do not know about the suffering of the poor and needy in our own towns and around the world. We learn of these things from television programmes and newspapers. Christians also know that the care of the needy was an important theme in Jesus' teachings.

Be careful not to use this passage in a question that asks for Jesus' teaching on the topic. It is a good example of how people react to Jesus' teaching and put it into action.

### 2A  *Acts 4: 32–7. Barnabas and the early Church*

The early Church took the words of Jesus and put them into action, as many individuals and organizations do today. They shared everything they had among each other and no one went without. The passage gives an example of the generosity of one early Christian. Barnabas sold a field and brought the money to Jesus' apostles to be given to those in need. This is the ideal Christian community.

## Try these short questions

**a**  Explain one reason why famine occurs. (2 marks)     (NEAB, 1996)

**b**  Explain what the parable of the sheep and the goats teaches Christians about their duty to those in need. (3 marks)     (NEAB, 2000)

## Exam-type questions

**a**  Name one country where famine is a constant problem. (1 mark)     (NEAB, 1996)

**b**  'Worshipping God at Mass is more important than helping those in need.' Do you agree? Give reasons for your answer, showing that you have thought about more than one point of view. (5 marks)     (NEAB, 1999)

## Student's answer

a  A country where famine is a constant problem is Ethiopia.

b  Of course worshipping God at Mass is important. God deserves to be praised for his goodness and mercy and a Christian enjoys doing this. During Mass a Christian can also receive the body and blood of Jesus. But at the end of the Mass the priest says, 'Go in peace to love and serve the Lord.' One of the ways a Christian can serve the Lord is to help the poor and needy in the world. Many people have so much to be thankful for and they should share what they have with those who have nothing. Jesus taught that Christians should help those in need.

## Examiner's comments

a  The student has given a correct answer.                                    Mark: 1/1

b  The student has started well. The importance of worshipping God at Mass has been explained. The point about the statement at the end of Mass is also valuable. However, what follows is rather vague. Yes, Jesus did teach his followers to help the poor and needy but the student has given no examples of this teaching. Examples of Bible passages the student could have used are given in this section. This omission would have cost the student two marks.        Mark: 3/5

## Examination practice

a  What is the difference between short term aid (emergency aid) and long term aid? (2 marks)

b  Name a Christian voluntary agency which helps those who need short and long term aid. (1 mark)

c  Some Christians do not wish to work abroad. How might they help people in poor countries? (3 marks)

## Checklist for revision

| | Understand and know | Need more revision | Do not understand |
|---|---|---|---|
| I understand the difference between the North and South. | ☐ | ☐ | ☐ |
| I understand the four main causes of poverty. | ☐ | ☐ | ☐ |
| I know the difference between short term aid and long term aid. | ☐ | ☐ | ☐ |
| I can describe the work of one Christian agency in the fight against poverty. Examples include short and long term aid. | ☐ | ☐ | ☐ |
| I can give examples of the teaching of Jesus and the early Church on the topic of helping those in need. | ☐ | ☐ | ☐ |

# 26 Christian values

## Topic summary

- The Ten Commandments, given to Moses by God, provide the basic rules for living a good life with God and fellow human beings.
- **2B** The Sermon on the Mount in Matthew's Gospel contains a number of important Christian teachings. They show the attitude and personality God wants in his people – the ideal Christian character.
- **2B** In his teachings, Jesus added to the old Jewish Law, which included the Ten Commandments. He taught that merely obeying the Law is not enough. Surface obedience to God's wishes is not what he requires; it is what is in the hearts and minds of people that matter.

Christian **traditions** number the commandments slightly differently. Catholics tend to join the first two commandments of one God and not worshipping idols together, but split the final commandment of not coveting your neighbour's possessions and spouse into two. Other Christians list the commandments as they appear in Exodus 20.

## What do I need to know?

- The meaning of the Ten Commandments and their relevance for today's society. The difficulties of observing the Commandments today. (Exodus 20: 1–17)
- The teaching contained in the Sermon on the Mount and the relevance of the Beatitudes for today's society. (Matthew 5–7; Matthew 5: 1–12)

## The Ten Commandments  2A  2B

The Ten Commandments give important guidelines as to how people should treat God and other people. For many societies, they provide the basic rules of good and moral living. Jesus showed the importance of the commandments when he told the rich young man he must keep the Ten Commandments if he wished to inherit eternal life (Matthew 19: 16–30).

The commandments can be divided into two groups. The first three concern a person's relationship with God, the remainder a person's relationship with other people.

### You shall have no other gods before me. You shall not make for yourself an idol

This commandment teaches that there is only one God. He alone deserves praise and obedience. When the commandments were given to Moses, the **worship** of idols, or statues, was common. Nowadays, people have other things that can become idols to them, such as the love of money, possessions, pop or film stars. The commandment says that people should not value material things or people more than they value God.

### You shall not misuse the name of the Lord your God

God's name should not be used lightly or without reverence. Those who swear with the words 'O God' or 'O Christ', are showing a lack of respect for God and His Son; their names should be treated with reverence and love. When making an oath or a promise, God's name should be used only if the intention is to keep that promise.

## Remember the Sabbath day by keeping it holy

God is deserving of praise and time should be devoted to him. Sunday, the Christian **Sabbath**, should be kept as a time to worship God and to rest. Although 'quality time' with God is important at any time, one day free from the pressures of work gives people the opportunity to spend more time with God and their families.

## Honour your father and your mother

Christians believe that family life is important. Respect should be given to those who lead the family unit. It enables them to carry out their responsibilities and it brings peace into the home. Respect, or honour, also shows gratitude and love to those who gave us life. Christians believe in God as Father; by honouring their parents they are, in turn, honouring God.

## You shall not murder

Christians believe that all human life is precious and a gift from God. No one, other than God, has the right to take that life away. Many Christians see this commandment as also referring to abortion, suicide and capital punishment. Human life should be respected; violence towards another goes against the will of God.

## You shall not commit adultery

For many Christians, marriage is a sacrament blessed by God. Promises of faithfulness to one's partner made at a marriage ceremony are intended to be life-long. Those who commit adultery bring pain to their partner and abuse their trust.

## You shall not steal

If something is not a person's to begin with, they have no right to take it. In modern society, stealing also includes non-payment of debts, fraud and the false claim of benefits.

## You shall not give false testimony against your neighbour

This commandment states that God's people are not to lie, spread rumours or damage the good name of another person. The truth must always be told.

**beware**

Some students wrongly say that Jesus' instruction, 'love your neighbour as yourself' (Matthew 22: 39) is one of the Ten **Commandments** – it is not!

## You shall not covet your neighbour's house or belongings

God's people should not be jealous of the possessions of others. They should be content with the blessings God has given them. Envy or jealousy of another's possessions can lead to thoughts of stealing; it also damages relationships with others. Christians believe that, in God's eyes, a wrong thought is as bad as a wrong action. This also applies to the final commandment.

## You shall not covet your neighbour's wife

It is God's commandment that his people should not long for those they cannot have. Coveting someone's spouse may lead to thoughts of adultery, thereby breaking the sixth commandment.

# The Sermon on the Mount  2B

In Matthew 5–7, the Sermon on the Mount comes at an early stage in Jesus' ministry. Jesus' role was to teach people about his Father and his Father's kingdom and make it possible for people to become members of that kingdom. In the sermon, Jesus concentrates on how God's kingdom differs from an earthly kingdom and the behaviour and attitude of those who are members of the kingdom of God.

Jesus used the list of rules his listeners understood – the Ten Commandments. He then went on to show that mere obedience to the Law of Moses is not enough – it is a right attitude that matters. Attitudes and actions based on love of God and of others, rather than token obedience to a list of rules, will result in correct behaviour.

## The Beatitudes

The Beatitudes (Matthew 5: 1–12) list those people who are blessed by God. Jesus speaks of righteous people – those who are morally good. The Beatitudes state that the righteous will not always be rewarded in this life – their reward will be in heaven. Jesus highlights those who are particularly blessed by God, those who know that they fall short of the expectations of God, the meek, those who are merciful to others, the pure, the peacemakers and those who are persecuted for their beliefs.

> **read more**
> Make sure you are familiar with those who are blessed by God in the Beatitudes.

The Beatitudes give a code of behaviour and right attitudes, which are valued and rewarded in the kingdom of God. There is a difference between the values and expectations of this world and those of God's kingdom.

## Other teachings from the Sermon on the Mount

- Salt and light (Matthew 5: 13–16)

    Christians must be like salt to the world. Salt is necessary for life. It also enhances the flavour of food. Christians must bring life to others. They are also the light of the world, guiding others to God.
- The importance of the Jewish Law (Matthew 5: 17–20)

    Jesus made it clear that he had come to complete the Jewish Law found in the Torah, not destroy it. The commandments must be obeyed and respected, as following them brings eternal life. But blind obedience is not enough – there must also be the right attitude and motive.

- Murder (Matthew 5: 21–6)

  Jesus taught that anger at another person can be as destructive as murder. Christians should make peace with those they have argued with before taking Holy Communion at Mass.

- Adultery (Matthew 5: 27–30)

  Jesus said that sometimes thoughts can be as bad as actions. If a married person lusts after someone other than their partner, then adultery has been committed in the mind.

- Divorce (Matthew 5: 31–2)

  Jesus stated that the only grounds for divorce is adultery. Divorced people who remarry are committing adultery as the promises of faithfulness made at the first marriage were meant to last a lifetime.

- Oaths (Matthew 5: 33–7)

  Christians should be so reliable and honest that they need not swear oaths to prove their honesty. Their word should be enough.

- Revenge (Matthew 5: 38–48)

  Christians must avoid the temptation to take revenge for wrongs done to them. They must be forgiving to those who have harmed them and make peace with their enemies. An important teaching in this passage is, 'Be perfect, therefore, as your heavenly Father is perfect' (v. 48). This is impossible for humans, but, in aiming to be like God, a person's life, actions and dealings with others are improved.

On punishment and forgiveness, pages 120–5.

- Charity, prayer and fasting (Matthew 6: 1–18)

  Jesus stated that God dislikes hypocrisy. God does not welcome good actions which are performed for the wrong reasons. Jesus gave three examples of good actions – charity, prayer and fasting – and said that an obvious show of these is not acceptable to God. They should be done quietly and without fuss, as good acts should be done for others and not to gain respect and praise for ourselves.

- Treasures in heaven (Matthew 6: 19–34)

  Jesus said that a person cannot love both God and money. A good relationship with God is far more valuable than money and possessions, which can easily be lost. Obviously, money is necessary, but it should not become more important than one's love of God or other people. Also, Christians should not be overly worried about having enough food to eat or clothes to wear. They should trust in God who will provide for the needs of his children.

- Judging others (Matthew 7: 1–5)

  Jesus said that his followers should be careful in the way they judge other people. If they judge others severely for wrongs done to them, then, in turn, God will judge them severely for the wrongs they have done. If they are merciful, God will be merciful to them.

- Ask, seek, knock (Matthew 7: 7–12)

  God is a loving Father. He wants the best for his children and prayers are not always answered how we would expect. Christians should pray for their own needs and the needs of others and trust God to answer prayer wisely and lovingly.

**hints and tips**

For revision purposes, make a list of the characteristics of a Christian, as mentioned in Matthew 5–7.

● The Christian life can be difficult (Matthew 7: 13–27)

This final section of the Sermon on the Mount is a warning to those who want to follow Christ. It is easier to sin than resist temptation. Following Christ sometimes leads to persecution and mockery. But the Christian way is the way to eternal life. The parable of the wise and foolish builders teaches that those who build their lives on the teachings of Christ have a foundation that will remain firm when problems and temptations arise.

## Try these short questions

a   In the Beatitudes, how will God help those who mourn? (1 mark)

b   Jesus said that Christians should be like salt and light. What did he mean? (3 marks)

## Exam-type questions

a   One commandment is 'You shall not steal'. Why is stealing considered wrong by Christians? (3 marks)

b   Some Christians find it too hard to follow the Ten Commandments in today's world. State and explain the reasons that they might give. (4 marks)                    (NEAB, 2000)

### Student's answer

a   The commandments give Christians direction on how they should live with God and other people. Stealing something that belongs to another person is wrong. It causes loss to that person – loss of the things that were stolen and loss of a feeling of security. A thief causes harm to another person and this is against the will of God. Christians should be grateful for the things God has given them. Stealing also goes against Jesus' commandment of loving our neighbours as ourselves – it is certainly not loving our neighbours to steal from them.

b   The commandments were given to Moses by God thousands of years ago. Times have changed a lot since then. Money and possessions are far more important to people now than they were in Moses' day. Some Christians might say that putting God first in their lives is too difficult because of all the pressures of work and family life. Also, there is so much media attention surrounding pop and film stars today that it is difficult not to idolize them. After all, we can see them to idolize and we cannot see God – sometimes he seems so far away and irrelevant to modern life.

## Examiner's comments

**a** This is a good answer. The student has identified the purpose of the commandments and has shown why stealing from another goes against the will of God. A link has also been made between the Ten Commandments and Jesus' two great commandments. Mark: 3/3

**b** The student has given several good points. For example, the fact that the commandments were given a long time ago and that society has changed since. However, the student was wrong to state that possessions are more important today than they were thousands of years ago – possessions and status have always been important. In a sense, the student has covered three of the Ten Commandments – those to do with God. There is no real reference to the difficulty of following the commandments concerning the way Christians treat others. Mark: 2/4

## Examination practice

**a** One commandment is 'Do not worship idols'. Explain how this commandment can be broken by Christians today. (2 marks)

**b** In the Sermon on the Mount, what did Jesus teach about the making of oaths? (2 marks)

## Checklist for revision

| | Understand and know | Need more revision | Do not understand |
| --- | --- | --- | --- |
| I know how Jesus respected and honoured the Ten Commandments and how they can be divided into two groups. | ☐ | ☐ | ☐ |
| I understand the meaning of each commandment and their relevance for modern Christians. | ☐ | ☐ | ☐ |
| I understand the relevance of the Beatitudes for modern society. | ☐ | ☐ | ☐ |
| I understand that the teachings contained in the Sermon show the right attitude a Christian should have towards God and other people. | ☐ | ☐ | ☐ |

# Answers to short questions

## 1 Background to the Gospels

**a** A binding agreement, a bond between God and his people.
(2 marks)

**b** The temple was the house of God. The Holy of Holies in the centre of the temple was the place where God was thought to be particularly present. The temple was the only place where sacrifices could be offered to God. (3 marks)

**c** They were a Jewish religious party. The name means 'separated ones'; they kept themselves apart from foreigners and from social outcasts. They taught and led worship in the synagogues. They spent much time explaining the Law and creating new rules about how the Law should be obeyed. (3 marks)

**d** Any one of the following: 'Talitha koum!' ('Little girl, I say to you, get up!'); 'Ephphatha!' ('Be opened!'); 'Hosanna!' ('Save now'); 'Abba' ('Father'); 'Eloi, Eloi, lama sabachthani?' ('My God, my God, why have you forsaken me?') (3 marks)

## 2 The person of Jesus

**a** Saviour. (1 mark)

**b** They believed he was the Messiah. The word means 'anointed one'. (2 marks)

**c** Give yourself up to 4 marks for your account of the healing of the Syro-Phoenician woman's daughter. Make sure you know and understand what they said to each other. (4 marks)

## 3 The suffering and death of Jesus

**a** They dressed him in purple. They put a crown of thorns on him. They mocked him, saying, 'Hail, King of the Jews.' They made Simon of Cyrene help to carry his cross. They offered Jesus wine mixed with myrrh. (Any two for 2 marks)

**b** 'My God, my God, why have you forsaken me?' (2 marks)

## 4 The resurrection and life after death

**a** In the next life, whose wife will she be? (2 marks)

**b** In the next life people do not marry; they are like the angels. In the Law it says that God told Moses that he was God of Abraham, Isaac and Jacob – all of whom had died. If the Law said he was their God, then they must still exist. (3 marks)

**c** If there can be life after death, then there is hope that death is not the end for Christians. They believe that they will share in the risen life of Jesus. (2 marks)

## 5 The kingdom of God

**a** The sower: the word of the kingdom is made available freely. People respond in different ways. Some accept the kingdom and lead others into the kingdom as well. (3 marks)

The wheat and the weeds: those who are members of the kingdom live in this life among those who do not accept it. At the Last Judgement, the members of the kingdom will enter heaven. (3 marks)

The yeast: the kingdom of God is a powerful influence in individuals' lives and in the world. (2 marks)

The pearl of great value: once people have realized how precious the kingdom is, they will sacrifice everything else to enter it. (3 marks)

**b** 'You are not far from the kingdom of God' was said to the lawyer who agreed with Jesus when he said the two great commandments were 'Love God and love your neighbour'. (3 marks)

'Let the little children come to me' was said to the disciples when they tried to stop people bringing children to Jesus. Jesus said that to enter heaven one has to become like a child. (3 marks)

## 6 Jesus' teaching on faith and prayer

**a** 'This comes only through faith and prayer.' (2 marks)

**b** He said that there was no need for Jesus to visit his house, he need only say the word. Jesus could give orders to diseases and evil spirits and be obeyed, just as the centurion's soldiers obeyed his orders. (3 marks)

**c** Because she believed so strongly in Jesus' power, she believed that touching his cloak would be enough to cure her. (3 marks)

**d** They must give her something to eat. They must not tell anyone. (2 marks)

## 7 Discipleship

**a** He called them to be fishers of men. He meant that, as they had drawn fish into their nets, they were to draw people into the kingdom of God. (3 marks)

**b** They were to tell people about Jesus the Messiah and Son of God and about the coming of the kingdom of God. (2 marks)

**c** Even though her gift was a small amount of money, it was a greater sacrifice than the gifts of richer people because it was a greater proportion of what she had. (2 marks)

## 8 Vocation and ministry

**a** Give yourself 2 marks for each of two examples such as: lead the worship, administer the sacraments, visit people for pastoral reasons, preach and teach, minister to the bereaved, conduct funerals, take an active part in the life of the community. (4 marks)

**b** They believe that all Christians can approach God themselves and that they do not need specially appointed ministers. Their worship may be spontaneous, with no appointed leader. All Christians are equal before God, with no need for leaders of a higher status. (4 marks)

## 9 The day of rest

**a** The Jewish holy day, the day of rest. It is from Friday sunset to Saturday sunset. (2 marks)

**b** He taught as someone with authority of his own, not like a teacher of the Law who had learned the teachings of someone else and was passing them on. (2 marks)

**c** He asked them whether it was right to do good or evil, to save life or to kill. His opponents taught that the Law had to be obeyed in every detail, even if it meant allowing people to suffer. He believed that it should be a day for doing good. (4 marks)

## 10 The Sacraments

**a** The leaders of the Church should pray over them and anoint them, and the prayer would save the sick; if they had any sins they would be forgiven. (2 marks)

**b i** Contrition: deep repentance, really being sorry for sins and resolving not to sin again.

  **ii** Satisfaction: an act to show a desire to atone, make up for sins. In the Sacrament of Reconciliation, the satisfaction may be the saying of a prayer, but it is said in the spirit of wishing to make good what has been done. (4 marks)

## 11 Holy Communion

**a** 'Take it; this is my body. This is my blood of the covenant, which is poured out for many. I will never again drink of the fruit of the vine until that day when I drink it anew in the kingdom of God.' (3 marks)

**b** It is the part of the rite when passages from the Bible are read, the main one being the Gospel, and the sermon (homily) is preached. (2 marks)

**c** Holy Communion: a bond with Jesus himself and with other Christians.

Eucharist: thanksgiving.

Mass: going out with a mission, with Jesus with them.

Lord's Supper: a meal at which Jesus is spiritually present. (4 marks)

## 12 Initiation rites

**a** They should baptize in the name of the Father, the Son and the Holy Spirit. (2 marks)

**b** In the Orthodox tradition, chrismation is the anointing of a child after baptism. Chrismation marks the seal of the Holy Spirit on the life of the child. (2 marks)

**c** Testimony is the public statement made by a candidate for believers' baptism, saying why that person has decided to be baptized. (2 marks)

**d** Candidates are considered old enough to be confirmed from about eleven onwards. In some Roman Catholic dioceses the age is a little higher. An examiner would accept any answer from eleven to about fifteen; 1 mark if your answer was within that range. That age is considered suitable because the candidates can understand and make a personal choice and commitment. (3 marks)

## 13 Sources of authority

**a** The Old Testament is from before the birth of Jesus. The New Testament contains the Gospels, accounts of the life and teaching of Jesus, and other writings of his followers. (2 marks)

**b** A statement of belief. (1 mark)

**c** The Son of God, conceived by the Holy Spirit, born of the Virgin Mary. (3 marks)

**d** Because she was the human mother of Jesus, God the Son. (2 marks)

**e** The authority to teach Church members what they should believe and how they should live their lives. (3 marks)

## 14 Places of worship

**a** It is the place from which the Word of God is preached. In the traditions in which the pulpit is the focal point, the Bible may be read and the whole service led from the pulpit. Its central position and the fact that it is usually raised reflects the importance of reading and preaching the Word of God. (3 marks)

**b** The iconostasis is a screen dividing the sanctuary from the area of the church where the congregation stand or sit. It has on it many icons, on which the worshippers may focus their attention to help them worship. The screen symbolizes the division between earth and heaven. At certain points of the service the priest comes through the Royal Doors, representing God coming to the people. (4 marks)

**c** The altar is the place at which the main action of the Eucharist takes place. The Eucharist is the main act of worship among Roman Catholics. (2 marks)

## 15 Pilgrimage

**a** A journey to a holy place. (2 marks)

**b** Give yourself 2 marks for each well made point, 1 for a weak point, to a maximum of 4. For example, they go for the spiritual experience of stepping from their everyday world for a time of focusing on their faith. They wish to visit and worship at places which are holy to them. (4 marks)

## 16 Prayer

**a** Meditation is focusing the mind on God and experiencing his presence. (2 marks)

**b** Extempore prayer is praying in one's own words. (2 marks)

**c** Liturgical worship is worship following a set formal pattern. (2 marks)

**d** An icon is an image, usually of Jesus or of one of the saints, which contains something of the nature and holiness of the person depicted. (2 marks)

## 17 Festivals

**a i** Christmas day. (1 mark)

  **ii** Because Jesus, the Son of God, took human nature. (2 marks)

**b i** His crucifixion. (1 mark)

**ii** Jesus died to atone for sin, to reconcile the human race to God the Father. (2 marks)

**c** **i** His resurrection. (1 mark)

**ii** The resurrection demonstrated that Jesus is the Son of God and that he won the victory over sin and death. Those who follow him can hope for heaven. (2 marks)

**d** **i** Pentecost (Whitsunday). (1 mark)

**ii** It marked the beginning of the Christian Church. They believe that the Holy Spirit has been active in the Church ever since. (2 marks)

## 18 Abortion

**a** The deliberate end, or termination, of a pregnancy. (2 marks)

**b** Adoption and fostering. (2 marks)

## 19 Voluntary euthanasia

**a** When someone suffering from an incurable and intolerably painful disease or injury states they wish to die with dignity. (2 marks)

**b** For: helping them to die will end their suffering, allowing them to end their lives with dignity.

Against: it goes against the commandment 'You shall not murder'. Only God has the right to take life away. (4 marks)

## 20 Conservation and stewardship

**a** Living in a 'throw-away' society encourages some people to think that resources are limitless. It shows a complete lack of concern for the world and the delicate balance of nature. (2 marks)

**b** **i** Genesis 2 teaches that God made humanity to be his stewards, to look after the world He had created. It should be kept in good condition for the next generation. (2 marks)

**ii** By looking after the world around them and ensuring they do no harm to the environment. This can be achieved by recycling, conserving energy and careful disposal of waste. A Christian can also take part in local initiatives to improve the area and join or support environmental groups. (3 marks)

## 21 Conflict, war and peace

**a** Jesus said they were making the temple into 'a den of thieves'. They were cheating people who worshipped there. (2 marks)

**b** All authority comes from God. Christians should obey authority, including their government's authority. (2 marks)

**c** They will be called sons of God. (2 marks)

**d** An evil person should not be resisted. The other cheek should be offered. (2 marks)

**e** **i** Someone who believes in peace and that war and violence are always wrong. All disputes should be settled peacefully.

**ii** Someone who uses extreme violence to achieve what they want, often killing innocent people. (4 marks)

**f** The motive must be right; the decision must be made by a government; there must be a good chance of success; only force which is absolutely necessary should be used; civilians must not be attacked; it must be the final resort. (6 marks)

## 22 Crime, punishment and forgiveness

**a** Christians believe that God is a loving Father who forgives all who repent of their sins. He does so gladly and welcomes them back to him. In the same way, Christians should forgive those who have wronged them. (4 marks)

**b** The penitent thief. One of the thieves who was crucified alongside Jesus understood that he had done wrong and deserved his punishment. Jesus said, 'Today you will be with me in paradise.' As a result of his genuine repentance, he was forgiven. It is never too late to repent. (4 marks)

## 23 Marriage and divorce

**a** Christians believe that God made humans male and female so that they could fall in love and marry. The couple are joined together by God and he is present in their life together. Marriage is the right environment to raise children. (3 marks)

**b** What God has joined together should not be separated. Christians believe that marriage vows are made in the presence of God. It is a life-long commitment of love and faithfulness. (2 marks)

## 24 Prejudice and discrimination

**a** Prejudice means to pre-judge others; often based on ignorance or misunderstanding. Discrimination is an action affected by prejudice. (2 marks)

**b** Everyone is our neighbour, regardless of race or religion. Christians should help those in need, whoever they are. (2 marks)

## 25 Aid to developing countries

**a** Famine can be caused by war. Farmers may be forced to fight rather than grow crops. War may also prevent vital food supplies reaching those who need it. (Other examples include drought and natural disasters.) (2 marks)

**b** Christians believe that by helping those in need they are following the example of Jesus, whose life was devoted to others. By doing this it is as if they are helping Jesus himself. Those who help the needy will receive eternal life. (3 marks)

## 26 Christian values

**a** They will be comforted. (1 mark)

**b** Salt is necessary for life. Christians should be a source of life to others. Salt also enhances the flavour of food. Christians can bring joy to others. Christians should be like light, guiding others to God. (3 marks)

**Abortion** The deliberate termination, or ending, of a pregnancy. This usually takes place before the foetus is 24 weeks old

**Absolution** When a person is declared forgiven of sin by a priest following confession and penance

**Adultery** Intercourse where one of the couple is married to someone else

**Annulment** A ruling that a marriage never existed according to the Roman Catholic Church

**Aramaic** A dialect of Hebrew, spoken at the time of Jesus. Mark, in his Gospel, often quotes Aramaic words spoken by Jesus

**Atones** Reconciles; removes any barriers or obstacles that stop people approaching God. Christians believe the death of Jesus atones for human sin

**Beatitudes** Christ's eight sayings in the Sermon on the Mount concerning those who are blessed by God

**Blasphemy** Speaking disrespectfully and offensively about God; using God's name in an irreverent way; making out that one is equal with God

**Capital punishment** Execution, the death penalty; a punishment given in some countries to those who have committed the most serious of crimes, for example, murder

**Ceremony** A formal act of worship with a special meaning. Many festivals have special ceremonies associated with them

**Church** With capital 'C', Christian people. With small 'c', a building in which the Church meet for worship

**Commandments** Something that must be obeyed. In particular, the Ten Commandments given to Moses (pages 149–51) and the two great commandments taught by Jesus (page 36)

**Commission** A vitally important task which must be completed

**Conscientious objectors** People who will not fight in a war, objecting to the killing of others as a matter of conscience

**Congregation** People attending worship. The reason they are called a congregation and not an audience is that it is important that they join in the worship

**Consecrate** Make holy, set apart for God, in a particular way. In the Eucharist, many Christians believe that when the bread and wine are consecrated they become the body and blood of Jesus

**Covenant** A solemn and binding agreement between God and his people

**Creation** The act of causing something to exist. The account of the creation of the world by God can be found in the first book of the Bible, Genesis

**Creed** A summary of important beliefs

**Developing countries** Countries that are working towards the development of their economy, industry and standard of living. Such countries used to be called Third World Countries

**Disciples** People who learn from, believe in and follow a teacher or leader

**Discrimination** Prejudice in action; action resulting from prejudice

**Divine Liturgy** The name used among Orthodox Christians for a celebration of Holy Communion

**Dominical sacraments** Baptism and Eucharist, the two sacraments based on the commands of Jesus. He instructed his followers to baptize and to receive the bread and wine, his body and blood, in remembrance of him

**Environment** The conditions in which people and other living things develop and grow

**Evolution** The scientific theory that describes how all life forms are the result of a continuous adaptation to their environment

**Extinction** No longer existing; the end of a species

**Faith** Belief and trust so strong that it involves following the person in whom you place your trust

**Gentiles** People who are not Jews

**Gospel** One of four books in the New Testament describing the life and ministry of Jesus. The word Gospel means 'good news'

**Grace** A gift of God's power and love

**Holy** Dedicated to God

**Hymns** Religious songs sung during public worship

**Initiation** Admission to the Christian faith and Church membership

**Inspired** Guided by God

**Just war** A war that is justified. Certain conditions have to be met for a war to be regarded by Christians as a 'just war'. (See page 116)

**Kingdom of God** Wherever God is accepted as king. (Matthew usually has kingdom of heaven)

**Last Judgement** The time, when the world comes to an end, when the words and actions of everyone will be judged. Those who are accepted will enter the kingdom

**Liturgy** The original meaning is service, something done for someone else. The word is used for different parts of an act of worship. For instance, a Roman Catholic Mass includes the Liturgy of the Word and the Liturgy of the Eucharist

**Long term aid** Aid to help a community become self-sufficient

**Magisterium** The teaching authority of the Roman Catholic Church

**Malnutrition** Not having the correct nutrients in one's diet, to the extent that it affects one's health

**Meditation** A form of prayer in which a person aims to escape from distraction and to focus attention on God

**Messiah** The leader promised by God to the Jews. Messiah is a Hebrew word meaning 'anointed one'. The Greek word is Christ – so Messiah and Christ mean the same thing

**Miracles** Acts beyond the power of the human race

**Nuptial Mass** A Eucharist during which a marriage takes place, with the bride and bridegroom receiving communion

**Observance** The keeping of a festival

**Pacifists** People who believe that war is never justified, even in self-defence or with a good cause

**Parables** Stories used by Jesus that explain the kingdom of God by comparing it with an example in everyday life

**Penance** An action to show sorrow for doing wrong

**Pilgrimages** Journeys to a holy place. The pilgrimage is the journey as well as what happens when the place is reached

**Pollution** Damage to the environment resulting from unsafe disposal of waste material

**Prayer** Conversation with God

**Preaching** Teaching in a formal way during worship, explaining the scriptures, encouraging and guiding the congregation. The preacher's speech is called a sermon

**Prejudice** Pre-judgment; an unfair thought or opinion based on misunderstanding or lack of knowledge

**Psalms** Ancient songs used in worship. The Book of Psalms is in the Old Testament. The psalms were used in worship in Old Testament times. Christians use the psalms in their worship

**Rabbi** A Jewish religious teacher, whose authority was accepted and whose teachings were studied by others. The teachers of the Law (Scribes) passed on the teachings of the rabbis

**Reconciliation** The mending of the relationship between God and a sinner. This follows repentance and forgiveness

**Repent** Admit one's sins, feel genuinely sorry for what one has done wrong and resolve to avoid sin in future

**Resurrection** Returning to life, rising from death

**Rite** The set words and actions of a particular religious ceremony

**Sabbath** Saturday, the Jewish holy day; a day of rest, marking the day on which God rested after creating the world

**Sacrament** A means by which a Christian may access the grace of God

**Sacrifices** Offerings to God. Some sacrifices in the Old Testament were thought to atone for sin, to remove the barriers which sin placed between God and the human race. Jesus' death is the perfect sacrifice, which atones for sin once and for all

**Scriptures** Holy writings. For Jews, including Jesus and his followers, the scriptures are what Christians know as the Old Testament. Gospel writers quote from the scriptures to show that Jesus was the Messiah

**Short term aid** Aid to cope with an immediate need or emergency

**Soul** The part of a person's nature, which is conscious and has feelings, emotions and moral values

**Symbol** A sign or object used to represent something

**Synoptic** The Gospels of Matthew, Mark and Luke. Although each Gospel has its own characteristics, they give a similar picture of Jesus

**Terrorist** Someone who uses extreme violence to achieve what they want, even at the cost of innocent lives

**Testimony** A personal account of an individual's own religious experience

**Tradition** This word is used in two ways: **1** Denomination **2** A long established custom

**Vocation** A calling from God to follow a particular way of life as a way of showing love of God and neighbour

**Voluntary euthanasia** When a person suffering from an intolerably painful, incurable disease or injury states that they wish help to die with dignity. Also known as 'mercy killing'

**Worship** Praising and adoring God. Christian worship can be either private worship (on one's own) or public worship (with other Christians)

# Index

abortion 99-103, 150
adultery 124, 131-2, 150, 152
Advent 93
aid to developing countries 141-8
aids to prayer 89-90
Anglican Church, views of 100, 105, 131
Annunciation 13
anointing of the sick 59, 60-1
apartheid 137
Apostle's Creed 76-7
arrest of Jesus 23-5
Ascension 96
ascension of Jesus 31–2, 96
authority, sources of 74-79

baptism 15, 59-60, 67-70, 80
Beatitudes 151
Bible 10, 74-5
birth of Jesus 13-14
burial of Jesus 25-6

CAFOD 146
capital punishment 122-3, 150
charity 152
Christ 18-19
    see also Jesus
Christian Aid 145-6
Christian values 149-54
Christmas 93-4
churches 80-4
confirmation 59-60, 70-2
conflicts 114-19
conservation 108-13
coveting 151
creation 102, 108, 111
crime 120-6
crucifixion 25-6

day of rest 55-8
death
    Jesus 15-16, 17, 23-9
    life after 30-4
    rites 33
dedication 69
developing countries 141-8
disability prejudice 136, 137
disarmament 117
disciples and discipleship 47-51
discrimination 135-40
Divine Liturgy 65
divorce 127-34, 152

earth 35, 39
Easter 94-6
emergency aid 144
environmental issues 109-10
Epiphany 93-4
Eucharist 59-60, 62, 64-5
euthanasia 104-7
evil spirits 15, 17-18, 56
evolution 108-9

faith 17-18, 36, 42-6
false testimony 150
fasting 152
festivals 93-8
forgiveness 120-6
funerals 33

gender prejudice 136, 137

Good Friday 95
Gospels 6-12, 30-1, 75
great commandments 36
Great Commission 49

healing 16, 17-18, 19, 42-4, 56, 60-1, 124
heaven 35, 39, 152
Holy Communion 62-6
Holy Land 86
Holy Saturday 95

idols 149
initiation rites 67-73

Jesus
    faith and prayer 42-6
    in the Gospels 8-10
    kingdom 35-7
    person 13-22
    prejudice and discrimination 137
    resurrection 30-4
    Sabbath 55-6
    suffering and death 23-9
Jesus Prayer 90
Jews 6, 55, 137, 151
judgement 152
just wars 116

King, Martin Luther 138
kingdom of God 35-41

Last Supper 17, 62-3
Lent 94
life
    after death 30-4
    start of 100
liturgy 62, 64-5, 91
Lord's Prayer 36, 89, 125
Lord's Supper 62
Lourdes 85-6
Luke's Gospel 10

Magisterium 77
Mark's Gospel 8-9
marriage 59-60, 127-34
Mary 77
Mass 33, 62, 64
Matthew's Gospel 9
Maundy Thursday 95
meditation 88
Messiah 18-19
Methodists 65, 105
ministry 52-4
miracles of Jesus 16, 17-18, 19, 20, 42-4, 56, 60, 124
murder 150, 152

New Testament 67-8, 75
nuclear war 116

oaths 149, 152
Old Testament 74
ordained ministry 52-3, 59, 60
organizations 100–1, 105, 110, 130, 144-6
Orthodox churches 81

pacifism 114-15
Palm Sunday 95
parables 37-9, 123, 124, 138-9, 146–7, 153
parents, honouring 150

peace 114-19
penitence 124
Pentecost 96
pilgrimage 85-7
Pope 78
poverty 141-8
prayer 42-6, 88-92, 152
preaching facilities 80
prejudice 135-40
private worship 90
protests 115
public worship 90-1
punishment 120-6

Quakers 64, 70, 82, 91, 115

racism 135, 137
reconciliation 59, 60
reform, aim of 121–2
rejection of Jesus 20
religious groups 7-8
religious prejudice 136, 137
remarriage 131
repentance 121, 124
Requiem Mass 33
resurrection 30-4, 55
revenge 152
rites, death 33
Roman Catholic
    churches 81-2
    marriage ceremony 129-30
    Mass 33, 62, 64
    views of 77-8, 100, 105, 131
rosary 89-90

Sabbath 55-6, 150
sacraments 59-61, 128
Salvation Army 64, 70
Saviour, title of Jesus 17-18, 19
science and Christianity 109
Sermon on the Mount 151-2
sexual prejudice 136
sexual relationships 131-2
sin and sinners 49, 120, 124–5
social outcasts 49-50
Son of David 18-19
Son of God 14-16, 19
Son of Man 16-17, 19
stealing 150
stewardship of the world 108-13
suffering of Jesus 23-9
Sunday 55, 56-7

temptation 19-20
Ten Commandments 55, 102, 117, 123, 149-51
terrorism 116
titles of Jesus 14-19
Transfiguration 15
trials of Jesus 15-16, 23-5
Tutu, Desmond 138

values 149-54
vocation 52-4, 60
vows 128-9

war 114-19
Whitsun 96
Word of God 10
worship 75, 80-4, 88-92